Favourite Foods of the Famous

Favourite Foods of the Famous

Compiled by
Freda Riseman

BOOK CLUB EDITION

To my husband
who, when asked to name his favourite dish,
replied, 'My wife.'

THIS EDITION PUBLISHED BY
PURNELL BOOK SERVICES, LIMITED,
ST. GILES HOUSE, 49/50 POLAND STREET, W1A 2LG
BY ARRANGEMENT WITH ROBSON BOOKS LIMITED
COPYRIGHT © FREDA RISEMAN 1974

Illustrations by Agnes Molnar

Set in Great Britain by
Cold Composition Limited, Tunbridge Wells, Kent

Printed in Great Britain by Biddles of Guildford

Contents

Foreword

It's been a lot of fun collecting the recipes for this book, and learning the gastronomic secrets and favourite dishes of so many famous people — and trying out the recipes on my long-suffering family has given my own culinary capabilities a tremendous boost!

If your family treats new recipes with the same suspicion as mine does, you will find that you can fend off all criticism by casually mentioning that if it's good enough for Frank Sinatra or Princess Grace of Monaco or Elizabeth Taylor, then at least it's worth a try. This ploy is quite amazingly successful.

I would like to thank the distinguished contributors to this book, who showed such kindness and went to such great lengths to obtain the details of their favourite recipes. Their cordial response and good wishes for the success of the book — from which all Royalties are being donated to Child Resettlement in Israel — were most heart-warming.

Thanks are also due to my daughter Lea for her keen detective work in tracking down the addresses I needed, and to my children Pinny and Helen for helping me to check the manuscript.

I hope these recipes will make an interesting talking point, and that your family and friends will lavish compliments on your expertise in cooking the 'favourite foods of the famous'.

1974

Freda Riseman.

hors d'œuvres

Tito Gobbi

hors d'oeuvre salad

1 large red-green tomato
1 medium-sized mozzarella cheese
   (if you can't find mozzarella, you may
   use a soft milk-flavoured cheese)

1 leaf fresh basil
olive oil
salt and pepper
small anchovies or black olives

Slice the tomato and cheese very thinly. Place them alternately all round an oval dish adding a leaf of fresh basil between the two slices. Pour a very tiny thread of olive oil all over the centre of this beautiful garland and season with salt and pepper. In the centre of the dish, place small anchovies or black olives.

Serve this very Italian hors d'oeuvre with crunchy 'grissini'. Try it for lunch, with all my best wishes. (Serves 1.)

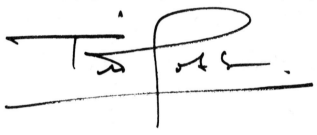

Mary Quant

mushroom hors d'oeuvre

½ lb large flat mushrooms
niçoise or provençal oil
black freshly ground pepper
few drops of tarragon vinegar

2 or 3 shallots
salt
parsley

Wipe the mushrooms clean — don't wash them. Chop them up and mix with oil and pepper. You will need a great deal more oil than you imagine and just a few drops of tarragon vinegar. Leave for 30 minutes to let the mushrooms absorb the oil. Taste — add more oil if necessary. Chop the shallots finely and toss in with the mushrooms. Add salt to taste. Sprinkle parsley on top. (Serves 4.)

Eat them!

8

Bernard Bresslaw

2 large bucklings
4 oz butter
2 tablespoons lemon juice
1 clove of garlic
salt
freshly milled pepper

smoked buckling paté

'This is a recipe which is not only a favourite of mine, but one which I — who have no pretensions to being a cook — can make with a high degree of success.'

Skin and bone the bucklings. This is easier to do if the bucklings are first dropped into boiling water for a minute or so — it's best to place them in a roasting dish and pour boiling water over them. Remove from the dish, slip the blade of a knife under the skin, and lift away first the skin, then lift the buckling flesh from the bone. Remove any small bones from the flesh with your fingers.

Using a wooden spoon, pound the flesh in a mixing basin with the softened butter. Beat in the finely chopped clove of garlic (with the papery coating removed) and the strained lemon juice. Season the paté with salt and pepper to taste. For a more delicate garlic flavour, simply rub the clove of garlic around the inside of the serving dish, then discard the clove.

If you have a liquidizer, blend for a few minutes to make a really smooth paté, then spoon it into a small covered dish and chill until ready to serve.

Serve with hot toast and butter.

Rita Tushingham

tush's toms

6 large tomatoes
4 hard-boiled eggs
a little butter
home-made mayonnaise to bind

salt
freshly ground black pepper
6 finely chopped spring onions
chopped parsley

Mash the hard-boiled eggs and mix together in a basin with the butter, mayonnaise, salt and pepper, until it is a smooth consistency. Add the finely chopped spring onions. Cut off the top of the tomatoes and scoop out the insides carefully. Fill up with the egg mixture, decorate with parsley — AND SMASHING THEY ARE TOO!

Sidney James

taramasalata

½ lb smoked cod's roe
1 small onion
1 clove garlic

½ pint olive oil
juice of a lemon
2 or 3 slices of white bread

Soak the bread in water and squeeze out surplus liquid with your hands. Remove the roe from the skin by scraping it with a metal spoon. Mix the roe and bread together in a basin and add the onion and clove of garlic finely chopped. Using a whisk gradually add the oil. When the mixture gets too thick pour in the lemon juice, slowly. Add more oil or lemon juice to taste.

Serve with hot toast or black bread.

10

Arthur Koestler
cocktail canapé

green peppers cut into one-inch wide strips

for the filling
taramasalata *or*
humus *or*
cottage cheese mixed with horseradish
tomato *or* cucumber slices for decoration

'This is a very simple hors d'oeuvre or cocktail canapé that I invented, and which is very effective.'

Fill the green pepper boats with any of the above fillings and decorate with tomato or cucumber. Season to taste.

Leslie Phillips
smoked salmon cocktail

1 small tin of sweetcorn, drained
2 oz smoked salmon pieces
6 orange segments, chopped
large dollop of good mayonnaise
    (preferably home-made)

one spoon of tomato paste or tomato ketchup
    to taste
shredded lettuce
pinch of paprika

Mix all the ingredients together and put in 4 glasses on a bed of shredded lettuce. Sprinkle a pinch of paprika on top of each glass to make it look pretty. (Serves 4.)

Norman Mailer

stuffed mushrooms

8 large mushrooms	grated nutmeg
1 large onion, chopped	breadcrumbs
2 shallots, chopped	cinnamon
chopped garlic cloves, to taste	grated lemon peel
salt and pepper	mustard powder

I take the mushroom stems and chop them finely. I add the chopped onions and chopped shallots and chopped garlic cloves. The nature of this dish is such that one can use more garlic than one would normally. Add salt and pepper to this mix, which is called *duxelles*. Add secret ingredient – freshly grated nutmeg. Sauté everything until brown. Then chill the mix for about an hour, at which point it's inserted in the mushroom caps and baked with a dusting of bread crumbs, cinnamon, grated lemon peel, mustard powder and a little more salt and pepper to taste. The baking need take no more than five minutes, and the dish should of course be served warm. (Serves 4.)

Hammond Innes

poached herrings

1 herring for each person	sliced dill cucumbers
fine onion rings	sour cream
sliced green apple	red pepper

'My wife serves this as a first course for summer dinner parties. We discovered it at Inigo Jones, and she promised always to credit them!'
Poach the herrings and remove bones carefully. Reassemble on the plate on which it will be served. Mix in a bowl the onion rings, apple and cucumbers. Combine with fairly thick sour cream. Pile this mixture on top of each filleted herring, enough to cover the fish. Sprinkle lightly with red pepper.

Violet Carson

plaice rolls

1 tin of sardines
8 level tablespoons fresh white breadcrumbs
2 level tablespoons finely chopped parsley
finely grated peel and juice of one lemon
1 level teaspoon finely grated onion

salt and pepper to taste
beaten egg to bind
1 oz melted butter
8 plaice fillets

Mash the sardines well and combine with the breadcrumbs, parsley, lemon peel, onion, salt and pepper. Bind loosely with the egg. Spread the sardine mixture over the plaice fillets and roll up. Arrange them in a buttered shallow heatproof dish. Coat the fish with the lemon juice mixed with the melted butter. Cover the dish with a lid or aluminium foil and bake just above the centre of a moderate oven for 30 minutes (M4-350°.) (Serves 8.)

Michael Bentine

cebiche de corvina

1 fillet of plaice, sole or any white fish,
    per person
1 onion, sliced
coconut milk or coconut oil

lemon juice
sweetcorn
Tabasco sauce

Soak the fillets (seasoned with salt and pepper) in the following mixture: sliced onions, coconut milk or coconut oil mixed with the lemon juice to taste. Soak for at least two hours and preferably overnight. This cooks the fish and it is similar in texture to a 'schmalz herring.' Lightly boil the sweetcorn and cut it into 1-inch thick slices. Place the sliced sweetcorn (which is called 'Choclo') round the fillet, and pour over a little Tabasco sauce to taste.

Dame Alicia Markova

avocado pear and grapefruit salad

1 avocado pear per person
1 grapefruit per person
1 tablespoon oil

1 teaspoon vinegar
pinch of sugar
fresh chopped mint

Cut the avocado pear and grapefruit into long sections. Cover them with a dressing of the oil, vinegar and sugar. Sprinkle over fresh chopped mint.

Graham Hill

avocado pear and orange

1 lettuce, washed and separated
1 avocado pear per person
1 orange per person

garlic
mustard
French dressing

Make a nest of the lettuce, then place slices of avocado pear alternating with sections of orange.

Serve with a French dressing highly seasoned with the garlic and mustard.

Harry Secombe

avocado and beetroot starter

4 oz cooked beetroot
2 oz celery
French dressing
2 medium-sized avocado pears

fresh lemon juice
salt
shredded lettuce leaves
2 hard-boiled eggs

Cut the beetroot into small dice and chop celery finely. Mix with the French dressing to taste. Halve avocados and remove centre stones. Sprinkle flesh with lemon juice and salt.

Stand avocado halves on individual plates lined with the lettuce. Fill avocados with the beetroot and celery mixture, then garnish with the hard-boiled eggs cut in quarters. (Serves 4.)

Norman Jewison

guacamole (avocado sauce)

2 large ripe avocados
1 medium-sized tomato, peeled, seeded
   and chopped
½ small onion, grated finely

2 canned serranto chiles, chopped
several sprigs fresh coriander, chopped
salt and pepper
pinch of sugar

Peel and mash avocados. Mix well with other ingredients and pile into a serving dish with an avocado pip in the centre. (This prevents avocado from turning dark.)

This is also excellent as a dip with fried tortilla triangles. (Serves 4.)

Norman Wisdom

spiced grapefruit

one half grapefruit per person
a little brown sugar
a pinch of mixed spice

a few drops of sherry (optional)
a few knobs of margarine
glacé cherries for decoration

'My taste varies from Irish Stew to Shepherd's Pie, but whatever the main course I always enjoy grapefruit served hot like this.'

Halve the grapefruit. Using a sharp serrated knife, cut it into segments and discard the pips. Sprinkle a little brown sugar over it, together with the mixed spice and the sherry if used. Dot it with small knobs of margarine, and cook under a medium heat grill for 4 or 5 minutes or in a pre-heated hot oven for 8-10 minutes (M6 — 400°) on the second shelf from the top.
Serve the grapefruit hot with a cherry in the centre.

David Kossoff

calf's foot jelly

2 calf's feet chopped into small pieces
cold water to cover
1 onion
1 clove garlic
3 bay leaves

a few peppercorns
salt and pepper to taste
2 tablespoons lemon juice
3 hard-boiled eggs
sliced lemon and parsley for garnishing

Cook the calf's feet in water for 10 minutes, skim and add the onion, garlic, bay leaves and peppercorns. Cook gently for one hour. Skim again and simmer for three hours or until bones stand away from the gristle and meat. Strain.
Cut the meat into cubes and mince. Add to the strained liquid and add lemon juice. Season to taste. Turn into a shallow dish and let cool until partly jellied. Put some slices of hard-boiled egg on the top and the remainder around the outside of the dish. Chill in the refrigerator. Garnish with the lemon slices and parsley. (Serves 6-8.)

cold soups

Barbara Cartland

'cool oasis' — cucumber and yoghurt soup

1 large cucumber
2 cartons plain yoghurt
2 tablespoons lemon juice
½ pint single cream
2 tablespoons double cream

'Culpepper in 1630 thought cucumbers were good for hot stomach and hot liver. He adds: "The face being washed with their juices cleanseth the skin and is excellent good for hot rheums in the eyes. It is also good for sunburning and freckles."

Yoghurt means long life; it also means important protein because yoghurt is partially digested. The valuable bacteria in yoghurt which live in the intestine help to destroy much of the gas and fermentation which can disturb us inside. Yoghurt is very important if you have been obliged to take antibiotics, which invariably kill many friendly and valuable bacteria in our intestine.'

Liquidize the cucumber and single cream together. Pour into a large bowl, stir in the lemon juice and yoghurt. Taste for seasoning. Chill for several hours and add the double cream just before serving. (Serves 2-3.)

Leon Uris

gazpacho (1)

1 small clove garlic
6 tomatoes
1 onion
1 green pepper
1 cucumber
6 tablespoons olive oil

4 tablespoons lemon juice
salt
cayenne pepper
¾ pint tomato juice
croutons

Remove the garlic skin. Blend 4 tomatoes and the garlic in an electric blender. Add ½ onion, ½ green pepper cut in rough pieces and ½ cucumber, peeled and cut in cubes, and blend. Pour mixture into a large tureen or bowl and chill. Just before serving blend together the olive oil, lemon juice, salt, cayenne pepper and tomato juice, and stir into above mixture. Serve with remaining chopped vegetables and croutons.

Peter Hall

gazpacho (2)

1 large tin tomatoes
1 small onion
1 clove garlic
2 slices white bread
4 tablespoons vinegar
6 tablespoons olive oil
1 chicken stock cube (optional)

½ pint water
½ green pepper
½ cucumber
2 tablespoons lemon juice
salt and pepper
sugar to taste
croutons for garnish

Put everything in the liquidizer and adjust seasoning. Serve chilled with croutons. (Serves 4.)

Peter Hall

Sadie Levine

gazpacho (3)

2 spring onions
half a peeled and sliced cucumber
2 tomatoes, cut in quarters
½ oz watercress
4 sprigs of parsley
1 tablespoon vinegar

1 tablespoon corn oil
7 oz tomato juice or half a can of juice
¼ teaspoon cayenne pepper
¼ teaspoon salt
garlic salt to taste (optional)
croutons or diced celery for garnish

'I get more accolades from guests for this extremely simple but sophisticated summer starter, than for all the rest of the dinner which is of course so much more complicated.'

Thoroughly blend all the ingredients together — except the tomato juice -- in a liquidizer. Place in a bowl and mix in the tomato juice. Serve with croutons or a sprinkle of diced celery. (Serves 4.)

Sir Isaac Wolfson

cherry soup

1 lb cherries
2½ pints water
4 oz granulated sugar

½ stick of cinammon
¼ pint single cream
1 tablespoon cornflour

Wash cherries and remove stalks and stones. Cover them with water and bring to the boil; add sugar and the cinammon stick. Simmer for 15 minutes then pass through a sieve.

Mix the cornflour gently with the cream, blend well and pour slowly into the soup. Simmer gently for another 5 minutes.

Serve cold. (Serves 6-8.)

Roman Polanski

chlodnik

1 lb cooked beetroot
2 pints water
1 teaspoon salt
2 teaspoons sugar
juice of 1½-2 lemons
1 hard-boiled egg
1 pickled cucumber
chives or green stems of spring onions
1 carton sour cream or 1 tub yoghurt

Peel beetroot and grate on a coarse grater. Add to the water and simmer with salt and sugar for 20 minutes. Only the liquid is used for the soup, so strain and discard the beetroot to use as a separate vegetable.

Add lemon juice to the liquid and allow to cool. Chop the hard-boiled egg coarsely, peel cucumber and slice it thinly, chop chives and add all these to the soup. Stir in the sour cream or yoghurt and whisk.

This soup should be served very cold, and will be pink in colour.

Kingsley Amis
avocado soup

2 large avocado pears (ripe to over-ripe)
1 small Spanish onion
juice of a lemon

pinch of chilli powder
a pint of creamy milk
salt (optional)

'The credit for this recipe belongs to my wife, Elizabeth Jane Howard, but since it's my favourite soup and I never tire of telling her so, she's allowed me to borrow it for this occasion. It's a perfect starter for a summer evening.'

Peel and roughly chop the onion. Scoop all flesh from the avocado pears and liquidize slowly with milk and chilli powder. Add salt if you like (I prefer it without), and the lemon juice. Pour into a jug, cover the top with a wet cloth and put in the refrigerator for several hours. (Serves 3-4.)

Kingsley Amis

Alan Whicker
quickie tomato soup

1 pint tomato juice
1 pint chicken stock
1 large onion, sliced
1 stick celery, chopped
6 peppercorns

½ teaspoon sugar
1 tablespoon lemon juice
salt and pepper
lemon slices for decoration

Put all the ingredients except the lemon juice into a saucepan and simmer gently for 15 minutes. Strain, add the lemon juice and season to taste. Serve cold with thin slices of lemon, twisted. (Serves 8.)

Crown Princess Marie Aglaë von und zu Liechtenstein

bulgarian tarator

2 cucumbers
salt
4 slices of white bread without crusts
small cup milk
1 garlic clove
½ pint of yoghurt
3 tablespoons oil
freshly ground pepper

'This is a yoghurt soup which is cold, refreshing and healthy.'

Peel the cucumbers and slice them very thinly. Salt the slices well and let them stand for an hour. Soak the bread slices in the milk. Crush the garlic clove in salt and blend with the yoghurt, oil and soaked bread. Liquidize this and add to the thoroughly drained cucumber slices. Refrigerate for several hours.

Just before serving sprinkle with fresh ground pepper. (Serves 3-4.)

Chaim Bermant

borscht écosse

1 lb beetroots
4 pints of water
one lemon
acetic acid
sugar
salt and pepper
½ pint sour cream
4 eggs
a little cucumber
a few radishes and spring onions

'This borscht will feed a family of twelve for a week, or a family of six for a fortnight. You needn't worry about deterioration. If your family will keep, the borscht certainly will.'

Wash and peel the beetroots. Cut into small pieces and simmer in salt water to which you add a little acetic acid to taste. When the beetroots are tender, take them out, grate them and return to the liquid. Add the sugar, salt, pepper and lemon juice to taste.

Beat in the 4 eggs and continue beating over a low flame until the mixture (which must not be allowed to boil) thickens. Cool, add the sour cream and refrigerate.

Add a dash — or, if you're that way inclined, two dashes — of whisky. Serve with finely sliced cucumbers, radishes and spring onions.

A variant is to serve all the above without the whisky. A further variant is to serve the whisky without the above.

hot soups

Claudia Cardinale

courgette soup

1 lb courgettes
1 oz butter
1 large onion

2 vegetable cubes
1½ pints water

Melt the butter and sauté the sliced onion gently for 5 minutes, taking care not to brown. Slice the unpeeled courgettes and add to the onions. Stir in the vegetable cubes dissolved in the water, and simmer for 30 minutes. Liquidize. Season to taste.

Ted Ray

onion soup (1)

2 oz butter
1 lb onions
1 tablespoon flour
2 pints water

salt and pepper
4 slices buttered toast
grated cheese

Cut up the onions in small pieces and fry in butter. Add a tablespoon of flour. Keep turning the mixture until it becomes a golden colour. Add the water, salt and pepper and boil for about 20 minutes.

Place the slices of toast in a heatproof dish and cover with the soup. Top with grated cheese and serve. (Serves 4.)

Alternatively, add 4 slices of bread and simmer in the soup for 10 minutes longer. Pass soup through a sieve and serve with cheese sprinkled on top.

Lord Shinwell
onion soup (2)

2 large onions
1½ oz butter
1 pint milk and water mixed
1 oz flour

pepper and salt
2 oz grated Cheddar cheese
chopped parsley

'I can only say that I enjoy any kind of food that my wife puts before me, whether it is smoked salmon, shmalz herring, sausages, steak and kidney pie, gefillte fish and, when we can afford it, a bit of steak, but above all the soup she makes. Oh the ecstasy, what a soup! As I sit at the typewriter my mouth is watering, thinking of it.'

Peel and slice the onions. Put in a saucepan with a little of the butter and sauté for 5 minutes with the lid on, shaking the pan from time to time. Then add half the liquid and cook the onions gently until they are soft. Melt the rest of the butter in a pan, stir in the flour and gently cook for a minute; stir in the rest of the milk and water, then add the onions and their liquor. Season well with salt and pepper. Just before serving, sprinkle with grated cheese and chopped parsley. (Serves 3.)

Sophia Loren
pasta and potato soup

2 lb potatoes, peeled and cut into
   small chunks
1 carrot, peeled and diced
1 large tomato, peeled and sliced
a few basil leaves

a little olive oil
½ lb spaghetti
2 quarts of hot water
salt and pepper

Sauté the carrot and tomato together with the basil leaves and the olive oil for a few minutes, then add the potatoes. When you see that it is nearly cooked add half a pound of pasta (spaghetti is the best, broken into short pieces) then almost at the same time pour the hot water into the pan.

When the pasta is cooked and the soup is looking very thick but still runny, it is ready for the table. Season to taste with salt and pepper. (Serves 6.)

(This recipe comes from *Eat With Me* by Sophia Loren, published by Michael Joseph.)

Malcolm Muggeridge

1 onion
1 oz butter
3 sticks celery
1 pint vegetable stock
grated peel and juice of one lemon
white sauce made with 1 pint of milk
salt and pepper
1 egg yolk and 3 tablespoons cream
   (optional)

celery soup

'My favourite nourishment is soup, and one of my favourite soups is celery soup made as follows.'

Cut up the onion and lightly fry it in butter. Cut up the celery including some of the leaf and toss it in the frying pan with the onion. Add the vegetable stock and put it all in a saucepan. Add the juice and grated peel of the lemon. Put it all through a sieve or liquidizer.

Make a white sauce with the milk. Add the sieved celery and simmer together for 20 minutes. Season to taste.

Optional. Just before serving, stir in the egg yolk blended with the 3 tablespoons of cream.

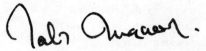

Donald Churchill

carrot soup

1 lb carrots, chopped
1 small onion, chopped
1 large potato, chopped
salt and pepper
a little sugar
parsley
butter
1 pint stock

'This is not a dish that has any immediate eye appeal, but it's very useful to men living on their own. It intrigues girlfriends with its taste, makes your wife rather loving because it's a meal she hasn't prepared herself, and it impresses mothers-in-law with its economy. And it's an ideal dish if you want something to "keep you going" until you have a full meal.'

Melt the butter and sauté the carrots, onion and potato. Add a little salt, pepper and a small lump of sugar, and mix together. Put lid on and leave on low heat for 15 minutes. Push it through a colander or wire mesh with a wooden spoon (I have used the bottom of a beer bottle!), leaving about 10% unsieved and still coarse. Keep this separate. Add a pint of stock and simmer on a low heat for another 15 minutes, then add the unsieved vegetables plus some finely chopped parsley. (Serves 3-4.)

Don't be tempted, if giving a dinner party, to make too much. For although the spirit of your guests may not be uplifted by the sound of carrot soup for starters, they'll always have more if it's offered, and so end up with no room for anything else!

Dame Sybil Thorndike

creamy carrot soup

1 lb carrots
1 large potato
1 onion
1 oz butter
¾ pint water
¼ pint of milk

1 oz washed rice
large pinch grated nutmeg
1 level teaspoon salt
2-3 tablespoons fresh single cream
2 teaspoons lemon juice

Coarsely grate the carrots, potato and onion. Fry gently in the butter in a saucepan for 5 minutes. (*Do not brown.*) Add the water, milk, rice, nutmeg and salt. Bring to the boil, lower heat and cover the saucepan. Simmer very gently for about half an hour.

When cool, stir in the lemon juice and cream. Re-heat without boiling.

Serve in warmed soup bowls.

Sybil Thorndike Casson

Nicholas Monsarrat

golden soup

1 medium onion, grated
1 medium carrot, grated
2 sticks of celery, chopped finely
   (*or* ½ teaspoon celery seeds)
1 medium to large potato, peeled and grated

2 tablespoons butter
1½ pints stock
½ pint milk
celery salt

Sauté vegetables in butter until limp but not brown. Add stock, bring to boil and simmer for half an hour. Add milk, re-heat, being careful not to boil. Add salt and pepper and a little celery salt to taste. Garnish with chopped parsley.

David Tomlinson

fish stew

1 lb haddock or other white fish
1 cup cold water
2 cups peeled, thinly sliced potatoes
3 tablespoons chopped onion

3 cups milk
1 tablespoon butter
salt and paprika to taste

Bone the fish and place in a saucepan with the water. Simmer for 10 minutes. Remove the fish and skin it. Replace the fish in the water. Add the potatoes, chopped onion and a little more water. Simmer for a further 10 minutes, then add the milk and bring to the boil. Just before serving add the butter and seasoning to taste.

Leo McKern

watercress soup

2 large onions
1 medium-sized carrot
2 lb potatoes
1 bunch watercress

1 teaspoon vegetable salt
2 pints stock
    (preferably home-made from shin of beef)
safflower oil or sunflower seed oil for frying

'My wife is vegetarian and wouldn't eat this, but she beautifully and cheerfully cooks it.'

Fry onion and carrot until soft and yellow — but not brown. Add to stock with the unpeeled, scrubbed and diced potatoes (either new or old.) Simmer until potatoes are soft, beat until vegetables are integrated, then strain through a sieve.

Add finely chopped cress. Heat (but do not boil) before serving. Season to taste.

Serve with croutons. Finely chopped green peppers sprinkled on at the last moment are a nice addition. (Serves 6.)

Golda Meir

chicken soup with knaidlach

for the soup
1 boiling chicken cut in quarters
water to cover
a little parsley
1 stick celery
2 carrots, peeled and finely sliced
1 onion, peeled and sliced
salt
pepper
a pinch of paprika
rice (optional)

for the knaidlach
2 matzos
1 onion peeled, sliced and fried
a little oil
some parsley
salt and pepper
2 beaten eggs
matzo meal

Cover the chicken with water and cook with the parsley, celery, sliced carrots, peeled onion, salt, pepper and a pinch of paprika for approximately 2 hours (or until the chicken is tender). If you like rice, you may add it after straining the soup. Wash it well and bring it to the boil in the soup for approximately 15 minutes.

I usually serve this chicken with knaidlach, which are made as follows: soak the matzos in cold water until soft, then squeeze dry. Crush with a fork and add to fried onions, the oil, parsley, salt, pepper and the two beaten eggs. Add enough matzo meal to bind. Make into balls and set aside for one hour. Drop the small balls into the boiling soup and cook for about half an hour.

fish

Sir Ralph Richardson

fillets of sole

8 sole fillets
1 oz butter
1 oz flour
¼ pint milk
1 tablespoon cream
pinch of cayenne pepper

salt and pepper
1 beaten egg
breadcrumbs
oil for frying
fried parsley for garnishing

Cut the sole into very small pieces. Make a roux with the butter, flour and milk. Add the sole pieces, seasonings and cream. Mix everything well together in a saucepan.

Turn out on to a dish and allow the mixture to cool before working into cutlet shapes. Dip the cutlets into the beaten egg, then the breadcrumbs and deep fry in oil.

Decorate the cutlets with fried parsley. (Serves 4.)

Ralph Richardson

Andrew Cruickshank

has no favourite recipe,
but offers this very useful advice:

Kippers. Put into *cold* water, bring to the boil and serve.
Herrings. Always best done in oatmeal, but never dusted too thickly.
Haggis. Prick and boil for at least 3 hours. Always serve with neat whisky. Never to be taken more than once a month.

All the above should be served on hot plates.

The Rt. Hon. Margaret Thatcher, MP

sole véronique

for the fish
4 large or 8 small skinned fillets of sole
white wine or wine and water to cover
6 peppercorns
1 small onion
1 bay leaf
1 tablespoon lemon juice
salt

for the sauce
1 oz butter
1 oz flour
top of milk or cream to make up to ½ pint

for the garnish
a few black grapes
chopped parsley

Butter a shallow ovenproof dish, fold the fillets in half and place in dish. Sprinkle with lemon juice, add the chopped onion, peppercorns and bay leaf. Cover with the wine or wine and water. Poach gently in a moderate oven for about 10 minutes (M5—400°.)

Skin and de-pip the grapes. Remove cooked fish, drain, wash the dish and replace fillets. Keep warm.

Strain fish liquor into small pan, boil quickly to reduce to 3 tablespoons. Add top of milk or cream to make up to ½ pint. Melt butter in pan, remove from heat. Add flour and stir until roux is smooth. Return to heat, add milk and stock, stirring well. Bring to boil and simmer a few minutes.

Check seasoning. Coat fillets with sauce, garnish with grapes and finely chopped parsley. Flash under grill to colour, or put back into the oven for a minute or two. (Serves 4.)

Ronnie Corbett

sole à la portugaise

for the fish
1½ lb dover sole or lemon sole fillets
2 teaspoons grated cheese
small finely grated onion
2 oz fresh breadcrumbs
a large tomato
1 beaten egg
a little butter
salt and pepper

for the tomato sauce
1 lb tomatoes (or 1 can tomatoes)
¼ pint of water
half a bay leaf
2 oz butter
½ teaspoon sugar
1 tablespoon tomato purée
1 oz flour
2 onions
salt and pepper
pinch of mace
1 teaspoon vinegar

Fish. Skin the tomato and mix to a pulp, then mix together with the breadcrumbs, cheese and grated onion. Season with salt and pepper and add sufficient beaten egg to bind. Spread each fish fillet with some of this mixture, then roll up tightly, beginning at the wide end of the fillet. Stand the fillets in a well-greased oven dish, and if there is any stuffing left over, roll this into small balls with floured hands and put in the dish. Dot these and the fish with butter, cover with greased paper and bake in a moderate oven about 20 minutes.

Sauce. Chop onions and fry in half the butter till lightly browned, then add the peeled and sliced tomatoes (or can*), water and half a bay leaf, and simmer for 20 minutes. Remove bay leaf and rub mixture through a sieve. Melt the remaining butter, stir in the flour, cook for a minute or two without browning, then gradually add the tomato purée. Stir till boiling, add the sugar, mace, salt and pepper to taste, and the vinegar. Simmer for 5 minutes.

When the fish has cooked, pour over the tomato sauce and serve. (Serves 4.)

*When using the can of tomatoes, omit the ¼ pint water in the sauce and use the juice from the can.

36

J. B. Priestley

sole marrakesh

for the fish
8 fillets of sole
8 oz patna rice
2 pints good fish stock
2 tablespoons white wine
a few dabs of butter
little salt

for the sauce
1 oz butter
1 generous dessertspoon flour
2 tablespoons cream
1 egg yolk

Cook the washed rice in one pint of stock, poach the fillets in the remaining pint of stock which has been lightly seasoned and mixed with the wine and butter. When fillets are cooked, drain off the liquid, cover the fish with buttered paper or foil, and keep hot. Reduce liquid to ½ pint by fast boiling. Melt the butter in a saucepan, stir in the flour and cook for a few minutes. Whisk in the hot stock. Mix the cream and egg yolk together, then stir it gently into the sauce. Season to taste.

Place the rice on an entrée dish, make a space in the centre for the fillets and pour a little sauce over. Serve the remainder of the sauce in a sauce boat. (Serves 4.)

Kenneth More

sole nature

2 sole fillets per person
milk to cover
1 large knob of butter

sprinkle pepper
pinch of grated nutmeg

'This is the quickest, simplest and tastiest dish in the world.'

Place the fillets in a Pyrex baking dish and *just* cover with the milk. Add the butter and sprinkle seasonings on top. Place in a hot oven for 7 minutes (M6—400°.)

Serve direct from the dish with very fresh French bread.

Terry-Thomas

sole san carlos

1 large sole

salt

Take a sole, prepare it for cooking leaving it in one piece. Put it into the pan on a bed of salt and cover with salt. Cook for 20 minutes on a moderate flame or heat — a little longer if it is a big sole.

This is all you do. You do not have to be a good cook for this to be successful, but you certainly have to be a good soul. (Serves 2.)

Marjorie Proops

for the fish
4 halibut steaks or 4 thick slices of
    cod on the bone
1 lb large onions
caster sugar and salt to taste
1 pint water

for the sauce
3 lemons
3 eggs
½ oz cornflour
1 teaspoon sugar
salt

sweet and sour fish

Slice onions in rings and boil in the water with seasoning for 30 minutes. Add the fish and simmer gently for a few moments until the fish is cooked. Remove onions and fish and strain the remaining fish stock. Put the fish steaks into a deep casserole and cover with the cooked onion rings.

Mix the cornflour to a smooth paste with the lemon juice. Beat eggs with one teaspoon sugar and a little salt, and pour slowly into the lemon juice paste. Add the fish stock gradually. Cook slowly, stirring gently until the sauce thickens. Add more sugar to taste. (Serves 4.)

Alan Sillitoe

bacalhau gomes e sa or suzette's bacalhau

1 lb bacalhau (dried salt cod)
1 lb potatoes
4 onions
6 tablespoons good olive oil
2 hard-boiled eggs
12 black olives, pitted
1 clove garlic
parsley
black pepper

This recipe calls for no salt, because there will be enough left in the bacalhau to salt the whole dish. Soak the bacalhau overnight, change water once. Put the bacalhau in fresh cold water, bring to the boil, and leave to cool in water. Remove skin and bones and flake fish. Boil potatoes in jackets. Slice and fry the onions and garlic in oil. Peel and slice cooked potatoes and eggs. All the cooked ingredients will now be assembled in a shallow casserole. Put in a layer of onion, a layer of bacalhau, a layer of potato, then repeat, ending with a layer of browned onions. Grind black pepper between the layers. Arrange the slices of egg and the olives over the top. Pour on a little extra oil as desired. Put in a low oven for half an hour. Sprinkle with chopped parsley. Serve hot. (Serves 4.)

Bobby Moore

halibut creole

4 large halibut steaks
2 large skinned and chopped tomatoes
1 small de-seeded and chopped green pepper
2 heaped tablespoons dry breadcrumbs
1½ oz melted butter
salt and pepper
pinch oregano
1 crushed clove garlic
1 tablespoon finely chopped onion
1 tablespoon grated cheese

'I must admit that I like only the basic simple foods; this is probably to do with the profession I am in. I am especially partial to halibut, and this recipe is really delicious.'

Toss the breadcrumbs in some of the melted butter. Cook the onions in the remainder till golden, then add the tomatoes and green pepper. Cook for two or three minutes until the butter has been absorbed.

Butter a shallow oven-to-table casserole and arrange the steaks in it. Spread the fried vegetables over the halibut steaks and season to taste. Cover with a layer of buttered breadcrumbs. Bake for half an hour near the top of a hot oven (M5−375°), until the fish flakes easily with a fork. Remove from the oven, sprinkle with grated cheese and brown under a grill. (Serves 4.)

Gracie Fields

savoury grilled cod cutlets

2 cod cutlets
2 tomatoes
1 lemon

1 oz butter
salt and pepper
sprigs of parsley

'My husband and I like simple dishes. Our favourite is a grilled sole, but in Capri it's difficult to find a fresh sole; we have a white fish grilled with tomatoes.'

Brush the cutlets and halved tomatoes with melted butter and season. Grill the fish for 5-7 minutes until lightly brown on both sides, and the cutlets are cooked through in the centre. Grill the tomatoes during the last 4 minutes of cooking time. Serve garnished with lemon wedges and parsley. (Serves 2.)

Jack Warner

herring savoury hot pot

2 lb potatoes, thinly sliced
½ lb onions, peeled and thinly sliced
4 fresh herrings, cut into fairly large pieces
2 beaten eggs

½ pint milk
breadcrumbs
a few pats of butter
salt and pepper

Grease a casserole dish and put in alternate layers of potatoes, onions and herrings. Season each layer, finishing with a layer of potatoes on top. Beat the eggs in the milk and pour over. Sprinkle with breadcrumbs and a few pats of butter. Cook in a hot oven for about an hour. (Serves 4.)

Dandy Nichols

for the fish
8 fillets bream
salt and pepper

for the stuffing
1 small onion, finely chopped
1 oz butter
1½ oz fine white breadcrumbs
6 oz grated cheese
1 beaten egg
1 level teaspoon paprika

for the garnish
sprigs of parsley
2 tomatoes

chinese stuffed fish

Skin the fillets and arrange 4 of them on a buttered ovenproof dish. Season with salt and pepper. Fry the onion in butter until soft, then mix together with the breadcrumbs, grated cheese, paprika, and bind together with the beaten egg. Spread half of the stuffing on the fish, cover with the remaining fillets, season and spread the rest of the mixture on top. Bake for 35 minutes at M5—375°. For the last 10 minutes of the cooking time, add the halved tomatoes to the dish.

Garnish with parsley and serve. (Serves 4.)

Wolf Mankowitz

for the fish
1½ lb haddock fillets
4 tomatoes, skinned and coarsely chopped
4 oz tuna fish
large can of new potatoes
chopped parsley

for the sauce
1 oz cornflour
½ pint milk
½ pint tomato juice
salt and pepper
grated rind and juice of 1 lemon

haddock and tuna fish casserole

Flake haddock fillets coarsely. Place in a shallow casserole dish with the tomatoes and the tuna fish. Add the can of potatoes. Blend the cornflour with a little water. Heat the milk and tomato juice, add the cornflour and stir over heat to thicken. Season to taste, and add lemon juice.

Pour sauce over fish. Cover with circle of greased greaseproof paper (or aluminium foil) and cook for 30 minutes at M5–375°.

Serve sprinkled with chopped parsley. (Serves 4-5.)

Chaim Topol

gefillte fish

2 lb fish (a mixture is best —
    haddock, cod, whiting, bream)
1 carrot, peeled
3 medium-sized onions
2 teaspoons salt
pepper
3 tablespoons white breadcrumbs
sugar to taste
2 beaten eggs

Get the fishmonger to fillet and skin the fish, but take the bones and skin. Wash the fish, bones and skin. Put the bones, skin and peeled carrot, one sliced onion, 1 teaspoon of the salt, pepper and a little sugar into a pan, and cover with water. Simmer gently for about 45 minutes.

Mince the fish together with the other two onions. Mix with the breadcrumbs, remaining salt, pepper, beaten eggs and one teaspoon sugar. With wetted hands, form into small balls and place them in the fish stock. Simmer gently for about 20 minutes. Remove the fish balls from the stock, place on a serving plate, and decorate with slices of the cooked carrot. Strain the stock, chill and serve separately.

If preferred, these fish balls may be fried instead of boiled. When you have formed them into small balls, roll them in white breadcrumbs and drop into deep hot oil. (Serves 6-8.)

Frankie Vaughan
herrings in oatmeal

1 large herring per person
oatmeal
salt and pepper

butter or oil for frying
parsley and lemon wedges for garnishing

Clean the herrings and split them open at the belly, then remove the backbone. Season coarse oatmeal with salt and pepper, then roll the fish in it on both sides. Heat the fat and when hot, fry the fish on both sides until golden.

Drain and serve garnished with parsley and wedges of lemon.

Ingrid Bergman
trout with cream sauce

for the trout
4 trout
juice of 1 lemon
a pint of thin cream
breadcrumbs
salt and pepper

for the garnish
lemon slices
chopped parsley
tomato wedges

Arrange the trout in a fireproof dish, add salt and pepper and the lemon juice mixed with 4 tablespoons water. Bake in a moderate oven (M4—350°) for 25 minutes.

Remove fish from dish and pour the liquor into a saucepan together with the cream, and reduce by half. Replace the trout on the dish and pour over the liquid. Sprinkle with breadcrumbs and brown in the oven. (Serves 4.)

N.B. To reduce liquid — boil in an uncovered saucepan on a very high heat in order to make the liquid more concentrated.

Moira Lister

golden plaice

4 large plaice fillets (skinned)
2 oz butter
lemon juice

salt and pepper
cornflake crumbs
mayonnaise (preferably home-made)

Sprinkle fillets with lemon juice and seasonings. Melt butter in a grill pan and grill the fillets gently for 5 minutes or till cooked. Baste occasionally with the butter.

Spread the fillets with a layer of mayonnaise and cover with crushed cornflakes. Baste with butter. Put back under the grill until the fish is golden brown and crisp. (Serves 4.)

Dulcie Gray

goujons of plaice

8 fillets of fresh plaice
1½ oz well-seasoned flour
1 egg
¼ lb fresh white breadcrumbs

for the sauce
mayonnaise (preferably home-made)
finely chopped chives, parsley, capers
  and gherkins

Skin the fillets. Cut into strips diagonally across the grain. Roll in seasoned flour, beaten egg and breadcrumbs. Roll the strips on a board under the palm of the hand. Deep fry in hot fat for 2-3 minutes until golden brown. Drain and serve with tartare sauce.

Roy Hudd

trout meunière

for the fish
6 rainbow trout
4 tablespoons plain flour
salt and pepper
1 oz butter.

for the sauce
1 oz butter
juice of ½ lemon
salt and pepper
1 dessertspoon finely chopped parsley
1 teaspoon freshly chopped herbs (*not dried*)

Wash trout and dry with absorbent paper. Roll them in the plain flour which has been seasoned with salt and pepper. Heat a heavy frying pan, drop in the butter, and when foaming, put in the fish and cook until golden brown on either side, turning once. (About 12 minutes in all.) Place the trout — without draining — on a hot serving dish and keep warm. Wipe out the frying pan with absorbent paper, add the butter and cook slowly to a nut brown. Add the lemon juice, seasoning and herbs, and while still foaming pour over the trout. Serve at once. (Serves 6.)

Michael Denison

worcester plaice

4 large fillets plaice

for the sauce
1 oz butter

1 oz flour
2 teaspoons tomato purée
4 teaspoons Worcester sauce

for the garnish
2 oz butter
1 small packet frozen petits pois

Put the fish fillets into a shallow pan, add water and seasoning. Bring to simmering point and poach for 5-10 minutes. Strain, retain the liquid and keep the fillets hot. Melt the 1 oz of butter, add the flour and cook for 1 minute without browning. Add the fish liquor, tomato purée, Worcester sauce and seasoning to taste. Bring to the boil, stirring all the time, and cook for 2 minutes.

Melt 2 oz butter in another saucepan, add peas and cook, tossing occasionally, for 5-10 minutes. Coat the fillets with the sauce and garnish with the petit pois. (Serves 4.)

meat and poultry

Elizabeth Taylor

haricots verts

2 lb French beans (fresh or frozen)
1 lb firm tomatoes, skinned and quartered
a little oil
2 bay leaves
3 sprigs of thyme
salt and pepper

'My favourite meal is the traditional Christmas dinner — roast turkey with a stuffing of finely chopped sausages and chestnuts mixed with breadcrumbs; brown giblet gravy, mashed potatoes, creamed onions, corn on the cob or sweet corn and haricots verts.'

Top, tail and wash the beans. Bring a pan of salted water to the boil, plunge the beans into the water, cover, and cook for 5 minutes. Drain beans in a colander. Melt the oil over a gentle heat, then place the beans in the oil, together with the tomatoes, bay leaves and thyme. Season with salt and freshly ground black pepper. Cover with a tightly fitting lid. If the lid is rather loose, place a greased round of greaseproof paper over the pan to hold it tightly. Simmer gently for about 15 minutes, shaking the pan occasionally. Remove bay leaves and thyme before serving. (Serves 6.)

50

Katie Boyle
roast turkey *(from Tony Stoppani)*

1 turkey weighing approximately 10-14 lbs
thyme and lemon stuffing

melted fat
chestnut mixture

'I love cooking and set out below one of my well and truly tested recipes for cooking the Christmas turkey in 1½ to 2 hours.'

Stuff the bird in the neck with the thyme and lemon stuffing. Leave the other end empty, making and serving your chestnut mixture separately. Brush or pour over the bird melted fat and place the bird in a pre-heated oven (M7—425°.) Baste often, cooking the bird until — when the baking dish is tilted — the juices inside run out clear like water. This is the most reliable gauge for the cooking time, however large the bird. I found a 16-lb turkey took just under two hours before the juices ran clear. Any longer cooking will only tend to dry out the turkey and make it slightly stringy.

Miriam Karlin
casseroled chicken

1 roasting chicken
1 clove garlic
pinch of tarragon and basil
1 tablespoon each dried green and red peppers
small glass of tomato juice

soy sauce
small wine glass red wine
½ lb button mushrooms
Chinese bean sprouts (optional)
seasoning

Skin the chicken. Place in casserole and season with garlic, tarragon, basil, salt and pepper; and add the dried peppers. Pour over the tomato juice mixed with a little soy sauce, together with the red wine. Cover with foil and place in a low oven (M1—250°) for 1½-2 hours.

Remove chicken from liquid and allow to cool. When the chicken is cold, quarter and bone it (these bones can be used another time to make a delicious stock). Place the boned chicken carefully in the casserole. Remove the top layer of fat from the liquid and pour over the chicken in the casserole. Surround with button mushrooms and Chinese bean sprouts and replace in oven for another 15 minutes. (Serves 4.)

Eleanor Summerfield

chicken with lemon sauce

for the chicken
6 chicken joints
2 medium onions, skinned and finely chopped
2 carrots, peeled and finely sliced
¼ lb mushrooms, sliced
a bouquet garni
salt and pepper

for the sauce
2 oz fat
2 oz flour
1 egg yolk
juice of half a lemon

Place the chicken joints in a large saucepan with just enough water to cover, and bring slowly to the boil. Take off the scum which rises, and then add the vegetables and bouquet garni, salt and pepper to taste. Simmer gently until the chicken is tender. When the chicken is cooked, remove the joints and keep them warm in a serving dish. Strain the stock and put it to one side, leaving the vegetables in the strainer for the time being.

In a medium-sized pan melt the fat, stir in the flour, cook gently for 2-3 minutes and remove from the heat. Measure off one pint of the strained stock (the rest will make a delicious soup) and gradually stir it into the cooked fat and flour. Bring to the boil and continue to stir until the sauce thickens. Add the vegetables and heat through for a few minutes.

Blend the egg yolk in a small basin and stir into it a few spoons of the sauce (this will prevent curdling.) Return this blended mixture to the sauce and heat through gently without boiling. Add the lemon juice.

Pour the sauce over the cooked chicken joints and serve with boiled rice and green peas, which add a nice touch of colour to the dish. (Serves 6.)

Valerie Singleton

chicken and pineapple casserole

4 roasting chicken joints
1 oz fat
12 oz can of pineapple rings
1 small sliced green or red pepper
3 tablespoons HP sauce or HP fruity sauce
1 chicken stock cube dissolved in one pint
   boiling water
1 level teaspoon flaked onions
salt
2 level teaspoons cornflour

'There is nothing tasteless about this chicken which is cooked with juicy pineapple and a spicy sauce. It is glamorous enough for a dinner party and very simple to prepare.'

Melt fat in a frying pan and brown chicken joints on all sides. Transfer to 4-pint ovenproof casserole. Add pineapple rings and juice, pepper slices, HP sauce, stock, onions and salt. Cover and cook for 1¼-1½ hours at M4—350°.

Remove chicken joints and pineapple rings to serving dish and keep warm. Blend about 2 tablespoons of cooking liquor with the cornflour in a small pan. Stir in remaining liquid, bring to the boil, stirring until thick. Check seasoning. Pour over chicken joints.

Serve surrounded with boiled rice. (Serves 4.)

Ned Sherrin

chicken parisienne

for the chicken
1 small roasting chicken
a bunch of herbs
¼-½ pint strong stock made from the giblets

for the mushroom sauce
1 oz fat
2 shallots
¾ lb button mushrooms
2 tablespoons brandy
salt and pepper

'This recipe has been slightly modified by my housekeeper, Miss Godfrey, to whom all credit is due.'

Season inside of the chicken with salt and pepper, put in the herbs. Place in a roasting tin, pour round the stock. Cook in a moderately hot oven (M6—400°) for about one hour, basting and turning from time to time. Meantime, prepare the sauce.

Melt the fat, add the finely chopped shallots, cover and cook for 2-3 minutes until soft. Add the sliced or chopped mushrooms and continue cooking for 3 minutes, then pour on the brandy and boil to reduce the liquid. Season to taste.

Take the chicken, carve it and arrange in a deep warmed serving dish. De-glaze the roasting tin with any remaining stock and boil down to one tablespoonful. Strain this through double muslin or a tammy strainer into the mushroom sauce. Pour the sauce over the chicken and serve. (Serves 4.)

Senator George McGovern

imperial chicken

1 chicken
3 cups breadcrumbs
salt and pepper

1 cup finely grated onion
½ cup melted margarine

Mix the breadcrumbs with salt and pepper and grated onion. Cut up the chicken into serving pieces. Dip the chicken pieces into the melted margarine, then in the crumb mixture. Arrange in a shallow roasting pan and dot generously with margarine. Bake for 1 hour at M4—350°.

N.B. Press the crumb mixture on to the chicken pieces, so that it is well coated.

Margaret Lockwood

chicken pilaff

1 medium-sized onion, sliced
left-over chicken, cubed
fat for frying

a little garlic
paprika
mushrooms, sliced

Melt the fat, sauté the onions and mushrooms, then add all the other ingredients. Season to taste.

Serve on a bed of rice.

Mike Yarwood

chicken in barbecue sauce

1 chicken joint per person

for the sauce
1 teaspoon Worcester sauce
juice of half a lemon
2½ oz can tomato purée

2 tablespoons brown sugar
½ pint water
1 onion, finely sliced
1 teaspoon salt
2 teaspoons mustard

Dip chicken joints in seasoned flour (flour mixed with salt and pepper) and fry in hot oil for a few minutes until golden. Drain well and place in a casserole. Put all the sauce ingredients into a pan and let simmer for a few minutes. Pour over the chicken joints, cover casserole, and place in the centre of a pre-heated oven (M4—350°) for 1 hour.

Spoon chicken joints on to a warmed serving dish. Skim fat from surface of sauce then pour sauce over joints. Sprinkle with chopped parsley to garnish.

Michael Barratt

roast lamb

for the lamb
shoulder of lamb weighing 4-4½ lbs
1 clove garlic
3 onions, thinly sliced
3 tablespoons flour
½ teaspoon salt
dash of pepper
⅛ teaspoon paprika

for the variation
2 carrots, quartered lengthwise
2 parsnips, quartered lengthwise
1 cup diced green pepper
1 cup diced white turnips
3 medium-sized skinned tomatoes,
  thinly sliced

Rub meat well with the cut clove of garlic. Arrange the onion slices in the bottom of the roasting pan and place the meat over. Combine the flour, salt, pepper and paprika and dust top of roast generously. Roast for 2 hours at M3—325° till nicely browned on top.

For the variation, roast the shoulder of lamb on a bed of all the vegetables mixed together, season to taste. Proceed as in basic recipe. (Serves 6-8.)

Richard Wattis

steak and liver pie

2 lbs chuck steak
½ lb ox liver
6 oz chopped onion
1 oz fat
heaped tablespoon flour

6 oz sliced mushrooms
Worcester sauce
salt and pepper
beef stock or 1 beef cube dissolved in water
pastry top

Cut steak and liver in cubes. Season and brown quickly in fat with onion. Stir in flour and cook for a moment or two. Add mushrooms, beef cube and enough liquid to make sauce like a thick cream. Season to taste. Transfer to a 2½-pint pie dish and cover with the rolled-out pastry top. Bake for 1½ hours at M2—300°.

Alternatively, pre-cook meat etc. for one hour. When soft, put on rolled-out pastry top and place in pre-heated oven (M7—425°) for 20 minutes until golden brown on top.

Professor Christian Barnard

veal scallopini with tomatoes

1½ lbs veal cut into 1-inch squares
flour mixed with salt and pepper
olive oil
½ lb thinly sliced mushrooms
½-1 clove pressed garlic

2 tablespoons chopped parsley
2 tablespoons chopped fresh basil
½ cup peeled, seeded, diced fresh tomatoes
½ cup Marsala
salt and pepper

Mix the cubes of meat with the seasoned flour and brown in the hot oil. Remove to an ovenproof casserole and add all the other ingredients. Season to taste. Cover and cook for about 45 minutes in a pre-heated oven (M3—325°.) (Serves 4.)

Roy Kinnear
escalopes of veal sauté à l'anglaise

5 veal escalopes
2 tablespoons flour seasoned with salt
   and pepper
1 beaten egg
1 fresh slice of white bread made into
   breadcrumbs

4 oz fat
tin of asparagus spears
juice of half a lemon
salt and pepper

Trim escalopes, dip them in flour, brush with beaten egg, then coat with the breadcrumbs, pressing them on firmly. Heat a large frying pan or sauté pan, put in half the fat, add the escalopes and sauté gently for 3 or 4 minutes on each side, until golden brown, turning once only. Take up escalopes and arrange in a warmed serving dish. Arrange the gently heated asparagus tips in the centre. Keep the dish warm. Wipe out sauté pan and re-heat the remaining fat to a noisette (nut brown) colour, then add the lemon juice with seasoning. Pour over the escalopes while still foaming, and serve at once.

Val Gielgud
veal escalopes in tarragon

4 veal escalopes beaten flat and thin
1 oz fat for frying
1 wine glass of dry sherry
salt and freshly ground black pepper

4 or 5 sprigs fresh tarragon (in winter when
   this is unobtainable, a smaller amount
   of rosemary is a reasonable substitute,
   although less delicate in flavour.)

'This recipe is a favourite of mine, and its merits are due to my wife rather than myself.'

Gently fry the escalopes in the melted fat for about 4 minutes each side and put in casserole to keep hot. Pour off most of any remaining fat, but retain pan juices and add sherry, stirring well. Bring to the boil and add tarragon, bruising leaves with spoon to extract flavour. Allow the liquid to reduce by half, then add salt and pepper to taste. Lower heat to a gentle simmer and put lid on pan to prevent further reduction. Simmer for 3 minutes, replace escalopes and warm through until really hot, then return to original casserole with the sauce. Plain boiled rice or well-mashed potatoes and puréed spinach go well with this dish. (Serves 4.)

Hylda Baker

1 lb stewing steak
1 stock cube
1 teaspoon HP sauce
1 large Spanish onion
4 large potatoes
a little oil for frying
1 large or 2 small bay leaves
half a tablespoon of Bisto
salt and pepper

lancashire hot pot

'I stayed in hotels for years and years, and certainly have personal preferences. As far as I am concerned, when I come home I like a homely dish — easy to make — I find it quite a change. When entertaining my theatrical friends to supper, with one voice they say: "Your Lancashire Hot Pot" so here is my recipe, for four people.'

Cut meat into cubes, slice onion and melt oil in a large enough frying pan or open saucepan and place in onions and meat. Stir around until reasonably browned, by which time the onions will have left some juice at the bottom of the pan. Stir the Bisto into some stock. Put the meat and onions into a deep casserole dish with a wide top, add the stock with enough water to cover the meat and onions. Add the bay leaf. Cover. Put the dish in a pre-heated oven (M6—400°). Leave to cook for about one hour, then give the meat a stir and pour in one teaspoon of HP sauce or similar, put in the potatoes then return to oven until meat is cooked and potatoes 'fall'. Season to taste.

Serve with peas and 'Pledge's Pickled Red Cabbage'! (Serves 4.)

Jimmy Tarbuck

tournedos steaks

4 tournedos
4 pieces of toast
¼ lb mushrooms
¼ pint red wine

for the sauce
2 oz margarine
1 oz flour
salt and pepper

'Tournedos are cut from the eye of the fillet of beef, and should be not less than one to one and a half inches thick. Though expensive, they have little or no waste, For an entrée, they are best cooked rare to medium to allow for the dish to be kept hot.'

Fry the steaks lightly, put one on each side of toast and keep warm. Fry mushrooms and place on top of the steaks. Melt the margarine, add the flour, stir in the wine, and bring to boil. Reduce to half. Season to taste. Serve the sauce over the steaks. (Serves 4.)

Cliff Richard

shepherd's pie

1½ lb cooked minced beef
½ lb finely chopped Spanish onions
a little olive oil for frying
½ pint rich beef stock
1 tablespoon Worcester sauce

1 tablespoon chopped parsley
¼ teaspoon mixed herbs
salt and pepper
1 lightly beaten egg
mashed potatoes

Sauté the onions in olive oil until transparent and soft. Add the minced beef and stock, Worcester sauce, parsley, mixed herbs, salt and pepper, and simmer gently for 2 minutes. Meanwhile add the beaten egg and a little melted fat to the cooked mashed potatoes. Place the meat in a deep well-greased casserole dish and cover with the mashed potatoes. Bake for 15-20 minutes in a hot oven (M6 or 7—400° or 425°) until golden brown. (Serves 4.)

Diana Rigg
beef goulash

½ pint cider
2½ lb cheapest cut stewing steak
1 lb onions
2 oz lard
1 tablespoon paprika

salt
2 tomatoes, peeled and de-seeded
1 or 2 crushed garlic cloves
grated rind of half a lemon
1 teaspoon of carraway seeds and dried marjoram

'As a change from ordinary cooking, I enjoy some international cuisine. Goulash is a stew using a cheap cut of meat, made tender by long slow cooking. The flavourings are unusual and result in a dish that is different and delicious. It re-heats well for a second day.'

Trim fat and skin from the steak and cut into strips. Cut the onions into thin slices. Melt the lard in a strong pan and fry the onion until golden brown. Stir in the paprika and half the cider and boil for a minute or two. Stir in the rest of the cider, the meat, salt, chopped tomatoes and seasonings (garlic, lemon rind, carraway seeds and marjoram). Cover pan with lid and cook as slowly as possible until the meat is tender (usually about 2-3 hours). Serve with boiled potatoes or plain boiled noodles. (Serves 6-8.)

Mike and Bernie Winters
minced meat bombs

for the minced meat bombs
2 lb minced beef
3 heaped tablespoons fresh breadcrumbs
1 large finely grated onion
1 egg lightly beaten
salt and pepper

for the sauce
1 medium-sized finely grated onion
small can of tomato purée
1 teaspoon lemon juice
1 teaspoon brown sugar
salt and pepper
½ pint stock or water

Mix the beef, breadcrumbs, onion, egg and seasoning together and form into small balls. Combine all the ingredients of the sauce into a saucepan and simmer gently for a few minutes. Drop the balls into the sauce and simmer gently for one hour.
Alternatively, place the balls in an ovenproof casserole, pour over the sauce, and cover. Place in a pre-heated oven (M4—350°) for approximately one hour. (Serves 6.)

Tommy Steele

thatched minced meat loaf

for the loaf
3 lb minced beef
3 eggs
2 large onions, peeled and finely grated
2 oz fresh breadcrumbs
2 oz margarine
1 tablespoon Worcester sauce
1 tablespoon tomato ketchup
1 beef stock cube, crumbled
seasoning to taste

for the garnish
3 lb boiled potatoes
thin slices of tomato
chopped parsley

Mix together the minced beef, 2 lightly beaten eggs, 1 of the finely grated onions, breadcrumbs, Worcester sauce, tomato ketchup, crumbled beef cube and seasoning. Turn into 2 greased loaf tins and bake for 50 minutes in a pre-heated oven (M4—350°) on the middle shelf. Meanwhile boil the potatoes and mash very thoroughly with margarine, the other grated onion, the third egg lightly beaten, and a little salt and pepper to taste.

After the loaf has been cooking for 50 minutes, turn out on to a heatproof serving dish and spread the potato mixture over the top and sides — using the prongs of a fork to form a 'thatched' effect. Return to oven for 25-30 minutes until golden brown, or brown under the grill on a low heat.

Serve hot with gravy, and garnish the meat loaf with the thin slices of tomato and chopped parsley. (Serves 8.)

The Rt. Hon. Jo Grimond, MP
chili con carne

1 lb minced beef
½ lb veal cut in 1-inch cubes
1 medium-sized onion
1 crushed clove of garlic
1 beef cube
salt and pepper

pinch of cumin powder and oregano
1 tablespoon chili powder (optional)
1 medium tin tomatoes
1 tin red kidney beans
½ tablespoon flour

Fry onions and add garlic and meats. Blend spices with flour and liquid from the tomatoes. Add to the meats together with the beef cube and tomatoes. Pour into an ovenproof casserole and simmer gently (covered) in a medium oven (M4—350°) for 1-1½ hours, until the veal is tender. Just before serving, add the drained kidney beans so that they are thoroughly warmed through. Serve on a bed of cooked rice. (Serves 6.)

Sir Bernard Delfont
hollishkes (stuffed cabbage)

for the stuffed cabbage
1 large cabbage (approximately 2 lbs)
1½ lb minced beef
1 large finely grated onion
2 lightly beaten eggs
salt and pepper
2 tablespoons fresh breadcrumbs
2 oz boiled rice (optional)

for the sauce
1 pint beefstock mixed with 2 tablespoons
  brown sugar
1 teaspoon lemon juice
1 small can tomato purée
salt

Blanch the cabbage leaves in a bowl of boiling water and remove the hard end of the stalk. Mix the beef together with the onion, eggs, seasoning, breadcrumbs and rice if used. Put a large spoonful into the centre of each cabbage leaf and roll up envelope fashion. Place in an ovenproof casserole. Pour over the sauce, cover the casserole and cook for about 3 hours in a very low oven (M2—300°). (Serves 6.)

Willy Brandt

farikal
(mutton in cabbage)

1 kilo mutton
1½ kilo white cabbage
1 teaspoon pepper
2 teaspoons salt
1½ tablespoons margarine (optional)
3 tablespoons flour
1 glass boiling water

'The best meat to use is from the front part of the animal. Mutton gives a better flavour than lamb.'

Prepare the meat by cutting it into equal portions. Coarsely grate the cabbage, discarding the hard white core. Place a layer of meat at the bottom of a heatproof dish. (If the meat is lean, dab a few pieces of margarine over it.) Put a layer of cabbage over the meat, and alternate the meat and cabbage layers — seasoning each layer with a sprinkling of flour, salt and pepper — ensuring that the top layer is cabbage. Be careful not to get any flour at the bottom of the dish.

Pour the boiling water over the layers, cover with a lid, and place in a moderate oven for 2-3 hours until it is golden brown in colour. Do not stir the dish while it is cooking, but shake it gently from time to time so that it does not stick at the bottom. When it is cooked, carefully place it on a hot serving dish — trying not to disturb the layers — and spoon the gravy over it. (Serves 4-6.)

salads

Susan Hampshire

sunflower salad

¼ lb button mushrooms
1 green pepper, sliced
a little chopped parsley
½ lb red cabbage, coarsely grated
1 apple

1 stick celery
a little onion salt
1 lemon
a little sunflower oil

In each of 4 small salad bowls put in a little of each of the mushrooms, green pepper, chopped parsley, red cabbage, apple and celery. Over each of the 4 bowls grind a peppermill 10 times. Take the onion salt and shake it around while counting five. Cut the lemon in quarters and squeeze a quarter dry over each bowl, using the flesh which drops out also. Add a little sunflower oil. This is a very good salad to eat with fish.

Millicent Martin

coleslaw

for the salad
1 lb crisp white cabbage
2 red dessert apples
juice of one lemon
2 carrots
1 green pepper
1 dessertspoon finely grated onion

mayonnaise to bind
1 teaspoon caraway seeds (optional)
salt and pepper to taste

for decorating
1 red dessert apple
juice of half a lemon

Discard the coarse outer leaves of the cabbage, cut in half and remove the thick stem. Shred finely and place in a bowl of ice-cold water for 20 minutes. Drain thoroughly. Cut apples into quarters, remove cores, slice thinly and sprinkle with lemon juice. Peel and grate the carrots. Cut the green pepper in half, discard stem and seeds, shred flesh finely. Mix prepared cabbage, apples, carrots and green pepper with onion and mayonnaise. Add the caraway seeds if liked. Season to taste. Decorate the edge of the bowl with thin slices of apple sprinkled with the lemon juice. (Serves 4-5.)

The Rt. Hon. Harold Wilson, MP
green salad

1 lettuce	¼ teaspoon salt
cress	pinch of pepper
finely sliced cabbage	¼ teaspoon dry mustard
watercress	¼ teaspoon sugar
a few finely sliced onion rings (optional)	1 tablespoon malt vinegar
a few slices of cucumber	2 tablespoons olive or salad oil

Wash the green vegetables and tear into pieces or slice, according to their type. Mix the seasonings in a salad bowl. Beat in the oil with a fork. Add the prepared salad ingredients and toss together gently for a few minutes, using salad servers. Mix the dressing with the salad ingredients just before serving. (Serves 4.)

Jimmy Young
continental salad

for the salad	*for the salad dressing*
2 medium-sized green peppers	2 tablespoons oil
1 lb tomatoes	1 tablespoon vinegar
half a cucumber	½ level teaspoon salt
	pepper
	½-1 level teaspoon concentrated mint sauce

Cut a slice from the stem end of peppers. Scoop out the seeds and pith, using a sharp knife. Cut into thin rings. Slice the tomatoes and cucumber thinly. Arrange in a serving dish with the pepper rings.

Mix all the dressing ingredients together well. Pour over the salad just before serving. (Serves 4.)

Caterina Valente

salade niçoise (1)

1 head lettuce
a handful of green olives
a handful of black olives
1 small can anchovies
3 hard-boiled eggs
2 red radishes
cooked green beans
1 onion
1 green pepper
chives
olive oil (8 tablespoons)
salt and pepper
4 tablespoons vinegar

Wash the lettuce in cold water, tear apart in not too small pieces and place in a salad bowl. Arrange the following ingredients in a nice pattern on top of the lettuce: the eggs cut lengthways, the black and green olives (keep back 6 of each for garnishing at the end), the chives and chopped onion, sliced beans and thinly sliced radishes.

Garnish salad as follows: arrange the drained anchovies in lattice fashion on top and put the olives in the holes. Combine in a separate bowl the olive oil, vinegar, salt and pepper to taste. Pour this dressing over the salad.

This salad can be used as an hors d'oeuvre or in summer as a main dish. (Serves 6.)

Bon appetit!

Dickie Henderson

salade niçoise (2)

for the salad
4 tomatoes, seeded and quartered
½ sliced Spanish onion
1 sweet green pepper, sliced
8 radishes
2 hearts of lettuce
4 stalks of celery, sliced
1 tin of tuna fish

8 fillets of anchovy
2 hard-boiled eggs, quartered
8 olives

for the dressing
2 tablespoons lemon juice
6 tablespoons olive oil
salt and freshly ground black pepper
12 leaves of fresh basil, coarsely chopped

Combine the prepared vegetables in a salad bowl, and place neatly on top the tuna fish, anchovies and quartered eggs. Dot with the olives. Mix the salad dressing and sprinkle over the salad. Serve immediately. (Serves 4.)

Yvonne Mitchell

salade niçoise (3)

1 cos lettuce
1 large tin tuna fish
18 black olives
4 hard-boiled eggs, halved
4 or 5 large tomatoes, thinly sliced

1 small tin anchovies in oil
a sprinkling of salad herbs
a few leaves of chopped basil
French dressing

'My favourite summer salad is a niçoise, but not arranged beautifully in layers as one sees it in England, simply tossed together in the real Niçoise fashion.'

Yvonne Mitchell

Anthony Quayle

crunchy carrot salad

1 lb carrots
1 lb dessert apples (preferably the red variety)

4 level tablespoons salted peanuts
4 level tablespoons mayonnaise

Peel the carrots and grate coarsely. Core and chop the apples (*unpeeled*). Mix together the carrots, apples and most of the peanuts. Add mayonnaise. Mix well and place in a serving dish. Sprinkle the remaining peanuts on top. (Serves 4.)

Benny Hill

tomato and courgette salad

6 courgettes
½ lb firm tomatoes
French dressing

salt and black pepper
a little chopped onion or chives

Plunge the courgettes in boiling salted water and simmer for 6-8 minutes. Drain well, cool and slice. Slice the tomatoes. Arrange on a serving dish, coat with dressing and season lightly with salt and black pepper. Finally sprinkle over the chopped onion or chives. (Serves 4.)

Joyce Grenfell

tomato salad

for the salad
½ lb tomatoes
a little sugar and salt
fresh chopped mint

for the French dressing (made in a jam jar)
sugar
a little oil
garlic vinegar
salt

To 1½ inches of sugar, add half an inch of oil and top them with 1½-2 inches of garlic vinegar. Add a little salt, stir well and keep in a sealed jar in a cool place, but not in a refrigerator. Put the tomatoes in boiling water to facilitate peeling. Peel and slice them thinly and put in a flat dish. On each separate slice drop a little sugar and salt to taste and a dab of French dressing. Chill and serve with the chopped mint sprinkled over all. (Serves 4.)

Joyce Grenfell.

Gayle Hunnicutt

poppy seed dressing

1⅞ cup sugar
1 teaspoon salt
1 teaspoon dry mustard
1 cup vinegar

3 cups salad oil (*never* olive oil)
1 very small grated onion
¼ cup poppy seed

'This recipe is delicious on fresh fruit salads or on green salads and is based on the famous Neiman-Marcus dressing.'

Mix the sugar, salt, dry mustard and vinegar together. Add the oil gradually, beating constantly, then add the grated onion. Add the poppy seeds and beat until thoroughly mixed. Makes 1 quart. This is how it is done 'by the book'. I actually put all these ingredients in the blender and blend at high speed for one minute, which works just as well.

Reg Varney

lorelei salad

½ lb cooked frankfurter sausages
1 can potato salad
1 tablespoon chopped chives

3 or 4 pickled walnuts
1 carton mustard and cress
1 jar pickled baby beetroots

Slice the sausages into rings and set a few aside for garnishing. Mix the remainder with the potato salad and chopped chives. Turn out on to a serving dish and garnish with slices of well-drained pickled walnuts and remaining slices of sausages. Surround with a border of washed and drained mustard and cress.

Serve with the pickled beetroots. (Serves 2-3.)

Muriel Spark

tomato mousse

3 hard-boiled eggs
½ pint cream
salt and pepper

8 oz jar tomato chutney (*not ketchup*)
½ oz gelatine
2 egg whites

Chop the hard-boiled eggs very finely. Whip the cream (not too stiffly), season and mix with the eggs. Add the jar of tomato chutney. Dissolve the gelatine in a very little hot water. Whip the egg whites very stiffly. Fold them into the mixture, add the gelatine, and pour into a soufflé dish. Chill. (Serves 6.)

Phyllis Calvert

cucumber mousse

2 cucumbers
one cup boiling water acidulated with a
    tablespoon lemon juice
1 teaspoon Worcester sauce
salt and ground white pepper
half a cup of mayonnaise
1 packet of gelatine
half a cup of cream
a little green colouring

'This is a delicious recipe which makes cold salmon more interesting. It can also be served with lettuce and cold hard-boiled eggs.'

Cut the cucumbers in half and discard seeds, leaving a little to be finely sliced and used as decoration. If the skins are tough, peel them. Blanch the cucumbers in a cup of boiling water acidulated with lemon juice for 5 minutes. Drain well and put them through a fine sieve or food grinder. Cool, and add one teaspoon Worcester sauce, salt and pepper to taste and the mayonnaise.

Soften the gelatine in a little cold water and dissolve it in a little bowl over a saucepan of boiling water. Mix well and add it to the cucumber mixture, together with the stiffly whipped cream. Blend well and add the colouring drop by drop.

Chill in a mould and serve decorated with slices of cucumber. (Serves 6.)

Alfred Marks

hot potato salad

3 large potatoes
2 onions, peeled and sliced
margarine mixed with a little butter for frying
2 eating apples, cored

salt and pepper
a little sugar
vinegar

Peel the potatoes and boil until barely tender. Drain. Fry sliced onions gently until they begin to soften but *do not brown.* Slice the apples, add to the pan, season well with salt, pepper, sugar and a dash of vinegar. Toss together until the potato is heated through and the seasoning is well distributed.

Max Bygraves

potato salad

1 lb cooked potatoes
1 small grated onion
1 finely grated hard-boiled egg
6 finely diced cocktail gherkins

a few finely sliced spring onions
salt and pepper
a little lemon juice
a little mayonnaise (preferably home-made)

Dice the cooked potatoes and mix well together with all the other ingredients. Bind with the mayonnaise and season to taste. (Serves 3-4.)

Julie Andrews
sunshine salad

4 large heads chicory
1 large bunch radishes
½ lb swiss Emmenthal cheese
2 dessert apples

strained juice of 1 lemon
4 oz shelled walnuts
a little French dressing

Cut the hard base from each head of chicory and remove the outer green leaves. Break heads into separate leaves and wash well. Trim and wash radishes well. Cut cheese into 1-inch cubes. Peel and core apples, cut into quarters, and sprinkle with lemon juice. Put chicory, radishes, cheese, apples and walnuts in a large bowl and toss in French dressing just before serving.

Bob Monkhouse
florida salad

½ lb mixed black and green grapes
2 oranges
2 bananas
a little lemon juice

French dressing
1 tablespoon fresh chopped mint
1 lettuce

Cut the grapes in half and remove the pips. Peel the oranges and cut into segments, discarding pith and pips. Peel and slice the bananas and sprinkle with the lemon juice to prevent discolouring. Toss the fruits with French dressing and mint. Arrange on washed, drained, lettuce leaves.

Simon Ward
simon's salad

2 large tomatoes
2 small cucumbers
1 small chilli pepper
1 sweet green pepper
1 small dill cucumber
1 small onion, finely sliced

2 cloves garlic, crushed
1 tablespoon chopped parsley
1 tablespoon mint, chopped (optional)
¼ cup olive oil
juice of 1 lemon
salt and pepper

Wash and finely chop all the ingredients and mix well with the oil and lemon juice. Season to taste. Place in the refrigerator until ready to serve.

Pete Murray
raisin and banana salad

1 lettuce heart
a little watercress
2 tomatoes, sliced
¼ lb cooked beetroot, sliced
1 onion, finely sliced

2 carrots, finely grated
a handful of raisins or chopped dates
2 bananas, finely sliced
2 large or 4 small jacket potatoes
    (boiled or baked)
cheese dressing

'This salad certainly delights me as a vegetarian.'

Mix everything together (except the potatoes) and pour over a cheese dressing.

Serve with boiled or baked potatoes. (Serves 2.)

cheese dishes

Peter Ustinov

cheese tart

shortcrust pastry to line a 7-inch flan case
2 beaten eggs
½ pint milk including the top of the milk

6 oz grated cheese
salt and pepper
pinch of cayenne pepper

Line a flan case with the shortcrust pastry and bake blind until the pastry is set but not too brown.

Beat the eggs with the milk, blend in the grated cheese and season with salt, pepper, and a cautious pinch of cayenne pepper. Turn into the pastry case and bake in a moderate oven (M4—350°) until set and golden brown (about 30 minutes). (Serves 4-6.)

Frank Muir

cheese scotch eggs

6 oz grated Cheddar cheese
1½ oz flour
1 level teaspoon salt
pinch of cayenne pepper
½ teaspoon Worcester sauce

1 beaten egg
2 tablespoons milk
4 hard-boiled eggs
browned breadcrumbs
oil for frying

Mix the grated cheese, flour and seasonings together, add the beaten egg and milk, and mix well. Using wet hands, coat the shelled hard-boiled eggs completely with the cheese mixture. Roll them in the breadcrumbs. Fry in hot deep oil for 2 minutes to allow the cheese mixture to cook through and brown. Drain, cool slightly, and cut across in half. (Serves 4.)

John Wayne
cheese casserole

2 cans diced green chillis
1 lb Jack cheese, coarsely grated
1 lb Cheddar cheese, coarsely grated
4 eggs

1 small can evaporated milk
1 tablespoon flour
fresh tomato slices

Separate the egg yolks from the whites. Beat the evaporated milk and flour in with the egg yolks, season with salt and pepper. To this mixture add the stiffly beaten egg whites, folding them in gently. In a deep ovenproof casserole which has been well buttered, mix the shredded cheese with the diced chillis. Pour the egg mixture over the cheese and 'ooze' it through with a fork. Place casserole in a pre-heated oven (M3—325°). Bake for 30 minutes. Remove from oven and place on top the slices of fresh tomatoes. Return to oven and bake another 30 minutes.

Dick Emery
dick's dish

for the dressing
1 tablespoon chutney
½ teaspoon sugar
1 tablespoon oil
1 tablespoon vinegar
½ teaspoon ginger
a little mayonnaise
   (preferably home-made), to taste

for the salad
1 small can pineapple chunks
1 small can peach halves
half a cucumber
2 large peeled and cubed carrots
8 oz Cheddar cheese
10 walnut halves

Cube the canned peach halves. Cut the cucumber into 1-inch wide rings, then cut each ring into 6 pieces. Cut the cheese into pieces and mix all together with the carrots, pineapple chunks and walnut halves. Toss the salad ingredients into a dressing made by mixing all the ingredients together. Adjust the seasoning to taste. (Serves 4-6.)

Denis Norden

cheese and
potato croquettes

1 lb cooked potatoes
½ oz butter
1 dessertspoon milk
salt, pepper and nutmeg
6 oz grated Cheddar cheese
1 beaten egg
browned breadcrumbs
deep fat or oil for frying

'Although I am to cooking roughly what Princess Grace is to Association Football, I do like the following dish.'

Mash the cooked potatoes with butter, milk and seasonings to taste. Add the grated cheese and mix together. Cool. On a lightly floured surface form mixture into a long sausage shape. Divide into about 16 croquettes. Coat with the beaten egg and then roll them well in the breadcrumbs. Repeat this a second time to get a good crusty coating. Fry in hot deep fat or oil until pale golden brown. Drain on kitchen paper and serve hot with tomato ketchup and a green vegetable, or cold with a salad. (Serves 4.)

The Rt. Hon. Jeremy Thorpe, MP

savoury camembert ice

4 oz Camembert cheese
1 tub cream

1 oz grated Parmesan cheese
cayenne pepper or paprika

Mix the Camembert cheese and cream together. Place in a small flat tin and freeze for 4 hours. Turn out and cut into fingers. Roll each one into the grated Parmesan cheese and decorate with a sprinkle of cayenne pepper or paprika.

Serve with hot crackers and butter. (Serves 2-3.)

Hermione Baddeley

gratin niçoise

1 lb courgettes
8 oz cooked rice
2 oz butter
2 peeled and mashed tomatoes
2 beaten eggs

6 oz grated cheese
salt and pepper
a little nutmeg
breadcrumbs

Top, tail and slice courgettes but *do not peel.* Cook in boiling salted water till tender. Drain and mix with the cooked rice. Melt butter, add the tomatoes and warm through, then mix in the beaten eggs, cheese and seasonings to taste. Mix all the ingredients well and place in an ovenproof dish. Top with breadcrumbs and dot with butter. Cook for 30 minutes at M6—400° until golden brown. (Serves 4.)

Sir Terence Rattigan

cauliflower cheese

1 medium-sized cauliflower
1 oz butter
1 oz plain flour
½ pint milk (or milk and cauliflower water)
3 oz grated Cheddar cheese

½ level teaspoon salt
1 level teaspoon made mustard
pinch nutmeg
1 oz extra grated cheese
1 tablespoon brown breadcrumbs

Soak the cauliflower in cold salted water for about 15 minutes then break into florets. Cook in a little boiling salted water in a covered pan until tender, drain and arrange neatly in a fireproof dish. Melt the butter, add the flour and cook for a minute. Remove from heat and stir in the milk gradually. Bring to the boil, stirring. Cook for a minute, remove from the heat, add the seasonings and grated cheese and stir until the cheese has melted. Coat the cauliflower with the cheese sauce. Sprinkle over the mixed grated cheese and brown breadcrumbs. Brown under a hot grill. Serve hot. (Serves 4.)

Sir Adrian Boult

cheese soufflé (1)

1 oz butter
½ oz flour
¼ pint milk
salt and pepper

a little mustard
3 eggs
1 dessertspoonful of breadcrumbs
2 oz grated cheese

Melt the butter in a saucepan, add the flour and cook together for a few minutes. Stir in the milk and heat gently to make a smooth sauce. Remove from the heat. Add the seasonings and the egg *yolks* one at a time, beat well, then add the breadcrumbs and cheese. Lastly fold in the stiffly-whisked egg whites. Pour mixture in a soufflé dish, cover lightly with a round of greased paper. Place the dish in a casserole containing a little hot water and cook in the oven for 50 minutes at M1—250°. Serve immediately. (Serves 3.)

Esther Rantzen

cheese soufflé (2)

1½ oz butter
1 oz flour
1½ gills milk
4 egg yolks
5 egg whites
2 oz each Parmesan and strong Cheddar cheese
salt
cayenne pepper
paprika
little extra grated Parmesan cheese
browned breadcrumbs

'I make this dish on very special occasions. It looks magnificent when it's well risen and brown on the top. It is quite impossible to eat in restaurants because they daren't risk hot soufflés. People rarely serve it at dinner parties because they think it will go flat, but I find that for supper parties it makes a lovely main course and if you keep the conversation and wine flowing it is possible to have it as a last course.'

Grease a soufflé dish. Melt butter in a saucepan, stir in the flour, add the milk and stir until boiling. Cool slightly and beat in the yolks one at a time. Season to taste, then work them into the cheese. Whip the egg whites stiffly, put a tablespoon of white into the cheese mixture and stir gently. Fold in the remaining egg whites. Turn mixture into soufflé dish and sprinkle top with a little Parmesan cheese and browned breadcrumbs. Cook in a moderately hot oven (M4—350°) for 25-30 minutes. (Serves 4.)

Edward Woodward

cheese and potato pie

8 oz grated cheese
2 lbs thinly-sliced raw potatoes
1 oz butter
just under ½ pint milk

salt and pepper
2 beaten eggs
¼ teaspoon nutmeg (optional)

Put alternate layers of grated cheese and thinly sliced potatoes into a buttered fireproof dish, ending with grated cheese. Melt the butter in the milk, season well and pour onto the well-beaten eggs. Pour this mixture over the potatoes and cheese, and sprinkle with nutmeg, if used. Bake in a moderate oven (M4—350°) for about one hour until the potatoes are cooked and the top nicely brown. Serve hot. (Serves 4.)

Sheila Hancock

cheese and sardine pizza

2 thick slices of toast and butter
2 sliced tomatoes
4 oz grated cheese

1 tablespoon Worcester sauce
small can of sardines
parsley

Arrange the sliced tomatoes on top of the toast. Mix together the cheese with the Worcester sauce and spread on top of the tomatoes. Place under a moderate grill until the cheese has melted. Arrange the sardines on top and return to the grill for 2 minutes. Serve hot, garnished with parsley. (Serves 2.)

Diana Dors

cheese moussaka

olive oil
1 large onion, finely chopped
salt and cayenne pepper
2 level tablespoons tomato purée
⅛ pint water
4 medium-sized aubergines
8 oz grated cheese

for the sauce
1 oz butter
1 oz flour
½ pint seasoned milk
salt and pepper

Heat the oil in a saucepan and sauté the onions. Season. Stir in tomato purée and water. Cover and simmer for 10 minutes. Peel and thinly slice the aubergines and lightly fry in a minimum of oil. Drain well. Put a layer of aubergines in the base of an ovenproof dish and sprinkle with some of the cheese, cover with a second layer of aubergines and cheese and season. Top with further layers, keeping back approximately 1 oz of cheese for the top.

To make the sauce, melt the butter, add flour and cook for a minute. Remove from heat and stir in milk gradually. Return to heat, bring to the boil, stirring. Cook for a minute, remove from heat, add seasonings and pour over top of prepared dish. Sprinkle with remaining grated cheese. Bake in a moderately hot oven (M5—375°) 20-30 minutes, until top is golden brown. (Serves 4.)

Henry Moore

parmesan puff

1 lb frozen puff pastry
1 well-beaten egg (Strained)
1 oz flour
2 oz grated Parmesan cheese
1½ oz butter
2 egg yolks
salt and pepper
7½ fluid ounces cold milk
2 tablespoons stiffly whipped cream

Roll out the pastry to ¼ inch thickness and cut a circle using a very large meat plate. Place on a wet baking sheet, brush top with the beaten egg and bake for 10 minutes at M5—375° then reduce the heat to M3—325° for a further 20 minutes. Cool on a rack and pipe the sauce on top.

Sauce. Place the remaining ingredients — except the cream — in a small pan and stir quickly and steadily over a low heat until the mixture boils and thickens and becomes smooth. Cool a little, then beat in the cream. This can be used hot or cold.

86

savoury supper dishes

Frank Sinatra

spaghetti
with tomato sauce

2 tablespoons salt
1 lb spaghetti
2 tablespoons olive oil
½ onion, sliced into very thin crescent wedges
1 tin peeled tomatoes
½ teaspoon pepper
½ teaspoon salt
¼ teaspoon basil
pinch of oregano
little parsley
4 cloves of garlic
grated cheese (optional)

In a frying pan heat the olive oil, add the onion and the 4 cloves of garlic. Sauté until brown and remove the garlic. Place the contents of the can of tomatoes in a blender with some of the liquid and mix gently for less than a minute. Slowly pour the tomatoes into the frying pan. Be very careful, because the liquid on the oil has a tendency to explode. Let this simmer for about 15 minutes, adding seasoning to taste, and stirring well.

While sauce is simmering, put the two tablespoons of salt into a large saucepan of water and bring to the boil. When the sauce is almost ready, put the spaghetti into the boiling water. Stir occasionally and when the spaghetti is done (test by tasting) pour it into a colander and immediately transfer to a heated serving platter.

Pour the sauce over the spaghetti and mix a little with two forks. Sprinkle some chopped parsley over the spaghetti and serve. Sprinkled cheese is optional.

Hot French bread and red wine complement this dish. (Serves 5-6.)

Henry Cooper
ravioli

for the dough
2 eggs
salt and pepper
pinch of ground ginger
flour

for the filling
mix together:
1 breakfast cup minced cooked meat
1 breakfast cup minced sausage meat
½ cupful breadcrumbs
2 teaspoons grated onion
salt and pepper
a beaten egg

Beat the two eggs with the seasoning and add enough flour to make a stiff paste. Knead thoroughly, roll out *very thin* on a floured board, and leave for a couple of hours to dry. Then cut into 3-inch squares. Put a teaspoonful of the mixed filling in the centre of each square, fold over into triangles, pressing the edges well together. Leave on a floured board for an hour or longer, to dry. Drop a few at a time into boiling salted water and cook steadily for 20 minutes. Drain thoroughly, put on a hot dish and coat with thick gravy.

Peter Sellers
ratatouille (1)

2 Spanish onions
2 green peppers
2 small red peppers
1 large aubergine
3 or 4 courgettes
1 can peeled tomatoes

lots of garlic
fresh chopped parsley
oregano
salt and pepper
oil for frying
chopped-up mushrooms (optional)

'I am a strict vegetarian and this is indeed my favourite dish.'
Slice the onions and simmer in oil until transparent. Dice the green and red peppers and add to the onions. Cook for 5 minutes. Add the diced aubergine (previously sprinkled with salt) and then the sliced courgettes. Simmer together for a few moments, then add the can of tomatoes, garlic, oregano and parsley, with salt and pepper to taste. Cover with a lid and simmer for 30 minutes.
If adding the chopped-up mushrooms, put them in 5 minutes before the end of the simmering period and they will be cooked just perfectly. (Serves 2-3.)

89

Alan Melville

2 fair-sized onions, chopped
4 medium-sized tomatoes
4 small (or two medium-sized) courgettes
2 aubergines
2 or 3 green peppers
clove of garlic
bouquet garni
salt and pepper
olive oil

ratatouille (2)

'*Ratatouille is a favourite Provençal speciality, prepared and eaten in vast quantities in and around Nice. It can be served hot or cold, is easy to prepare, and also makes an excellent first course. This is how the Niçois do it, and therefore how it should be done.*'

In a large frying pan simmer slowly in olive oil the chopped up onions. Add the tomatoes — peeled, crushed and with as many of the pips removed as you can be bothered to remove. (Fresh tomatoes, please, *not* tomato purée.) Add the courgettes, cut crossways into thin slices, then the aubergines, also cut up into small segments, and the peppers — with their innards removed — and again cut up into small pieces. Then and most important of all if you're feeling at all Provençal — a whole clove of garlic, the bouquet garni and the salt and pepper to taste.

Let the mixture (which now looks like a lady vegetarian's garden party hat) simmer slowly for at least half an hour, giving an occasional stir so that the ingredients get to know each other; also the occasional crush with a fork to the garlic clove and the bouquet garni just to add pungency to the dish.

It may take slightly less or slightly more than half an hour. At any rate, consider the operation completed when the juice from all the ingredients is just on the point of evaporating. Don't let it evaporate completely — keep the mixture slightly gooey. Whisk it off the heat and either eat it there and then, or put it in the fridge to be served cold on a hot summer's day. (Serves 4.)

Bon appetit!

Arthur Askey

ratatouille (3)

1 lb mushrooms
2 large onions
1 lb aubergines
1 large tin red peppers
1 lb courgettes
2 lb cooking tomatoes
2 tablespoons tomato purée
2 lemons
2 teaspoons cumin powder
3 cloves of garlic
½ cup of water
1 teaspoon sugar
salt and black pepper
oil for frying

'My favourite dishes are Moules Marinière, Liver and Bacon, and — believe it or not — TRIPE; but as the latter sounds as if I am eating my own material, I recommend this variation of Ratatouille.'

Chop the onions. Crush the garlic cloves in a little salt to form a paste. Warm the oil in a large frying pan, add the onions, garlic paste and cumin powder and simmer gently for about 5 minutes but *do not brown*.

Add the tomato purée and cooking tomatoes which have been peeled, de-seeded and sliced, and mix well. Gradually add the sliced mushrooms, sliced red peppers, sliced courgettes and the aubergines which you have cut into 1-inch squares.

Add the juice from the lemons, the water, sugar and black pepper, and simmer for 1½ hours — during which time you should taste for seasoning to see if you need further salt. (Serves 6-8.)

Princess Grace of Monaco

for the dough
1 lb white flour
15-20 grammes of yeast
1 glass olive oil
1 tablespoon warm water
a little milk
pinch of salt

for the sauce
3-4 onions
3-4 tablespoons tomato purée or
   4 fresh peeled tomatoes
oil for frying
anchovies and olives

pissaladière

'This is a local dish which is absolutely delicious.'

Dough. Pour yeast into a little water. Put flour in a bowl and make a well in the middle of the flour and pour in the creamed yeast, olive oil and salt. Knead the dough with a little milk until it comes away from the sides of the bowl. Let it rest in a ball until the dough has risen three quarters of its volume.

Sauce. Peel the onions and slice them thinly. Cook them in oil till golden brown. Add the tomato purée or fresh tomatoes. Mix well. Place the dough on an oiled plate, spreading to the thickness of 1 inch. Pour sauce over dough, adding a few anchovies and olives for garnish. Put in a moderate oven and cook for approximately 20 minutes to half an hour.

Serve cold. (Serves 4-6.)

92

Eamonn Andrews

baked potatoes and 'caviar'

for the potatoes
2 large potatoes per person, well scrubbed
salt and pepper
for the 'Caviar'
4 aubergines
2 medium-sized onions

3-4 dessertspoons of tomato purée
1 dessertspoon each of lemon juice and vinegar
black pepper
clove of garlic (optional)
sugar and salt to taste
oil

'Once I was the guest of a famous Puerto Rican actor in a plush London restaurant, and one of the dishes he gave me was a baked potato filled with caviar. Obviously the cost did not concern him that particular night, but he remarked: "Isn't it ironic to think that two famine items of nourishment now represent a very expensive dish — caviar that kept the Polish people alive in times of stress and potatoes that kept Irish people alive in times of national hunger." My favourite and most versatile dish is Baked Potato with practically anything, but the "Poor Man's Caviar" is most tasty. It can be used to stuff the baked potatoes or decorated with parsley and wedges of lemon and served with rye bread.'

Prick the potatoes with a fork to avoid an oven explosion and cook them at a steady heat (never lowered or the potato may become soggy) and when they are nice and crispy on the outside, break them open and pop in whatever you fancy — from chopped onion to whatever is handy — salt and pepper, and you have a dish fit for kings and commoners alike.

'Caviar.' Smear the aubergines with olive oil and bake in a very slow oven for two hours or until soft. Cut open and take the flesh out and chop finely. Sweat the onions in olive oil until transparent and add to the aubergines. Put the mixture in a saucepan and add the tomato purée, vinegar, lemon juice, black pepper, garlic, sugar and salt to taste. Cook slowly until all the liquid has evaporated.

Jack de Manio

chinese rice

3 lb cooked brown rice
1 lb fresh bean sprouts, chopped
½ lb fresh mushrooms, chopped

1 bundle spring onions, chopped
1 large packet frozen green peas
2 tablespoons soya bean oil

Heat the oil and sauté the bean sprouts and mushrooms. Pour into a large shallow overproof dish, and add the cooked rice and spring onions. Mix well together and season to taste. Bake for 30 minutes at M4—350°.

Steam the peas and serve with the rice mixture. (Serves 8.)

Artur Rubinstein

savoury potatoes

1 lb potatoes
1 oz melted butter

¾ lb smoked haddock, boiled and flaked
1 carton yoghurt

Boil and drain the potatoes and mix with the melted butter. Over this spread the boiled flaked haddock, then pour a carton of yoghurt over the dish. (Serves 2.)

Sydney Tafler

polish potato pudding

2 lb potatoes, peeled and coarsely grated
2 eggs
1 large onion, peeled and finely grated

salt
pepper
4 oz margarine

Drain the grated potatoes to remove excess moisture and mix lightly with the beaten eggs, onion, seasoning and melted margarine.

Transfer to a 2-pint pie dish and bake for approximately 1 hour at M5—375° until golden brown on top.

Serve hot. (Serves 5-6.)

Sydney Tafler

Mary Stewart

pommes de terre maison

1 lb potatoes
1 large Spanish onion
¾ pint beef stock

salt and pepper
1 oz margarine

Grease a 1-pint ovenproof dish with margarine. Peel and thinly slice the potatoes, slice the onion into rings and place in alternate layers with the potatoes in the dish, finishing with the potatoes, the layers overlapping.

Pour over this the beef stock which has been seasoned with salt and pepper, dot over with the margarine and bake in a moderate oven (M4—350°) for 30 minutes until the vegetables are soft and the stock has been absorbed. Serve piping hot. (Serves 4.)

George Cole

6 green peppers
8 oz minced beef
1 small can tomato purée
chopped parsley
¼ lb mushrooms
2 tablespoons cooked rice
salt and pepper
1 medium onion
½ teaspoon sugar
2 tablespoons water

stuffed green peppers

'I courted my wife with this dish and we still enjoy eating it!'

Discard stems, cores and seeds of green peppers. Rinse in water and let dry. Add 2 tablespoons water to the minced beef and mix well, adding some of the tomato purée, the chopped parsley, rice, salt, pepper and chopped mushrooms. Stuff peppers with this mixture. Arrange in an ovenproof casserole with the cut end uppermost.

Slice the onion, divide it into quarters and place a quarter slice on each pepper. Dilute the remaining tomato purée with water, and pour in the casserole until the peppers are almost covered. Add the sugar and a pinch of salt to this liquid. Cook for 35-40 minutes in oven (M4—350°.) (Serves 3.)

96

General Moshe Dayan

2 kilo pickled egg-plant
3 eggs
4 oz flour
2 carrots
2 onions
2 green peppers
1 clove garlic
½ cup sugar
juice of 2 lemons
1 cup water
1 tablespoon soy sauce
1 teaspoon monosodium glutamate
1 chilli pepper
½ cup tomato purée
1 tablespoon cornflour

for the garnish
fresh tomatoes
fresh lettuce

sweet and sour egg-plant

Cut the egg-plants in ½-inch pieces, dip in the beaten egg, then in flour, and deep fry. Drain on paper towelling. Place in a saucepan, add lemon juice, tomato purée, soy sauce, water and sugar. Bring to the boil and then add the cut carrots, sliced onions, green peppers and crushed garlic. Simmer for a few minutes (until the vegetables are soft) and then add monosodium glutamate, salt and pepper to taste, and the cut chillis. Let simmer gently for a few more minutes.

Just before serving, add the cornflour (pre-mixed in cold water to a smooth paste) slowly to the sauce. Place the fried egg-plants on a large serving dish — garnished underneath with fresh lettuce and with cut tomatoes in wedges round the egg-plant — then pour sauce over egg-plant and tomatoes.

Serve with rice. (Serves 10-12.)

Lulu
vegetable curry

2 oz margarine
1 chopped onion
1 chopped apple
1 tablespoon curry powder
1 tablespoon flour
1 pint stock or water
little lemon juice
1 dessertspoon dessicated coconut

1 tablespoon dried fruit
1 teaspoon sugar
1 dessertspoon chutney
salt and pepper to taste
1 lb mixed vegetables
   (beans, carrots, turnips, parsnips, etc.)
boiled rice (¼ lb per person)

Melt the margarine and fry the apple and onion until soft. Stir in the curry powder and flour, and cook for several minutes. Add the liquid and bring to the boil. Stir in all the other ingredients and simmer gently for 35 minutes. Serve with the boiled rice. (Serves 4.)

Donald Pleasence
no-name curry

1 teaspoon ground dhaniya
2 teaspoons ground turmeric
½ teaspoon chilli powder
1 tablespoon butter
½ teaspoon ginger
salt and pepper

ground garlic
½ pint milk
2 tablespoons cream
large tin of drained salmon
shredded coconut

Put dhaniya, turmeric and chilli powder into a saucepan, add the butter, ginger and seasonings. When the butter has melted, add the milk and cream, stirring until yellow. Add the tin of drained salmon, cooking gently for a few minutes. Pour into a casserole dish, and cook for another 15 minutes in the oven. Just before serving, sprinkle shredded coconut over it and grill until lightly brown. Serve with a bowl of rice. (Serves 4.)

Donald Pleasence.

Acker Bilk

meat curry

1 onion
1 apple
a little oil
1 tablespoon Vencat curry powder
1 level tablespoon flour
1 pint stock
1 tablespoon chutney
2 oz sultanas
8 oz cooked meat or chicken
salt and pepper
boiled rice
Green Label mango chutney

Peel and chop the onion and apple and fry in a little hot oil. Add the curry powder, together with the flour and fry gently for one minute. Blend in the stock, bring to the boil, add the chutney and sultanas and simmer for 30 minutes.

Dice the cooked meat or chicken and add to this sauce, season to taste and simmer very gently for a further 10 minutes.

Serve with boiled rice and Green Label mango chutney. (Serves 2-3.)

Val Doonican

colcannon

'This is a very popular dish in Ireland particularly on Fridays and is a must for Hallowe'en. It's very simply made with mashed potatoes and cooked greens, but if possible, with curly kale, using about half as much greens as potatoes, or as preferred. The method goes something like this—'

Peel and cook the amount of potatoes required. Mash very thoroughly. Cream well with a good knob of butter or margarine, pepper and salt and a little heated milk. Cook the kale or greens until tender. Drain and chop very finely. Add to the mashed potatoes which have been kept hot. Add a tablespoon or so of very finely chopped onion. Cream everything together and be sure to serve piping hot — with the butter dish near at hand.

Paul McCartney

egg and chips

1 lb potatoes   **2 eggs per person**
oil for frying

'I know this is hardly a Cordon Bleu dish, but it really is my favourite.'

Peel potatoes and cut across into thick slices, then into finger strips. Soak for a short time in cold water, then drain and dry thoroughly in a clean cloth. Heat fat or oil, place the chips in the frying basket and lower slowly. Fry till lightly browned, then lift out the basket for a minute or two, increase the heat of the oil, and return the chips for a few more minutes till crisp and brown. Drain and sprinkle with salt and pepper.

Serve with two fried eggs per person. (Serves 2.)

Anton Dolin

scrambled eggs dolin

4 eggs
1 oz butter

salt and pepper

Separate eggs and beat yolks with salt and pepper. Whisk the egg whites and gently fold into the yolks. Melt the butter in a saucepan and pour in the egg mixture. Keep stirring. Place in a hot dish and add a good pat of butter.

Serve with dry toast. (Serves 2.)

Pancho Gonzalez

beans and tortillas

'I am a Mexican and I have been raised on Mexican food, and as far as I am concerned, no one can make it better than my mother. My favourite dish is Re-fried Beans with Flour Tortillas and a nice cold glass of milk. I will try to remember how my mother made the beans.'

You take brown beans — making sure you sort the small pebbles out — then you boil the beans until cooked, then drain them. Incidentally, the juice from the beans makes good soup. Place the beans in a pan and mash them around, use butter or margarine and fry on a low flame. Place them on a serving dish, and be careful you don't burn your mouth.

Serve with tortillas, which you buy.

Pancho Gonzalez

Lady Antonia Fraser

english and irish quiche

for the quiche
8 oz packet of frozen chopped spinach
8 oz packet of frozen puff pastry
  (or make it yourself)
4 oz cream cheese
4 oz Cheddar cheese, grated
4 eggs, beaten
4 oz double cream
salt and pepper

for the tomato sauce
1 medium-sized onion
2 medium-sized carrots, grated
1 tin of tomatoes
garlic (either salt or fresh)
bay leaf
salt and pepper
butter

Roll out the pastry and line an 8-inch flan dish with it. Cook the spinach and let it cool. Mix the cream cheese and beaten eggs together, add the cream, salt and pepper, half of the grated cheese and the spinach. Pour into the flan dish and sprinkle the remaining cheese over the top. Put into oven M5—375° for 25-30 minutes.

Chop the onion and sauté in the butter, add the grated carrot, garlic, and continue to sauté for 5 minutes. Add the tin of tomatoes, bay leaf, salt and pepper. Simmer for 15 minutes or until the vegetables are cooked. Liquidize the sauce and reheat when needed.

Antonia Fraser

desserts

Gracie Fields

les pommes au four
(Baked apples if your French is dodgy!)

1 large lemon
6 large cooking apples (about 3½ lbs)
3 oz butter
3 oz shelled walnuts, coarsely chopped
4 oz soft brown sugar or ¼ pint clear honey
1 egg yolk
6 tablespoons water
4 level tablespoons apricot jam

Finely grate the rind from the lemon, then squeeze out the juice. Peel and core the apples, coat them in the lemon juice to prevent discolouration and place them in a shallow overproof serving dish. Melt the butter in a small pan and brush a little over the apples. Add the walnuts, brown sugar or honey, excess lemon juice and grated rind to the rest of the butter over a low heat.

Lightly whisk the egg yolk and stir it into the ingredients in the pan. Gently reheat without bubbling. Spoon the walnut sauce into the apple centres having hollowed them out a little more if necessary. Spoon 4 tablespoons water into the base of the dish. Bake at M6—400° for an hour, covering loosely with buttered foil when the apples are golden brown. Test with a skewer to ensure they're cooked.

Heat the apricot jam and 2 tablespoons water in a small pan and reduce until thick. Brush the apples with this glaze. They can be kept in the oven on a very low heat until ready to serve, just as they are or with lashings of double cream. Either way they're fabulous. (Serves 6.)

Gracie Fields

Cyril Fletcher

betty astell's ice cream

½ pint double cream
1 egg yolk
4 oz icing sugar
sugar roses and violets

1½ cups diced pineapple
two tablespoons peach or apricot brandy
1 stiffly beaten egg white
1½ cups thick whipped cream

Mix sugar and egg yolk till almost white and add the ½ pint of cream. No cooking is required. This should freeze in normal fridge freezer in about 3 hours. For a party when you want a really special sweet try a snowball.

Use the cream-based ice cream mixture and add to it the diced pineapple, peach brandy or apricot brandy and freeze it all in a round mould (a small pudding basin will do). When it has frozen, remove the basin carefully so as to keep the shape. Cover with 1½ cups of thick whipped cream to which you have added the egg white. Lift the mixture into rough peaks with a fork and decorate thickly with crystallized rose and violet petals. It's luscious!

Ludovic Kennedy

chocolate coffee ice cream

4 eggs
6 oz caster sugar
1 carton cream

2 tablespoons coffee
½ tub of chocolate spread

Whisk together the eggs and sugar for about 10 minutes in the mixer until it has more than doubled in bulk. Slowly add the coffee (dissolved in a little hot water) and the chocolate spread to taste. Fold in the whipped cream and freeze.

Eric Morecambe and Ernie Wise

individual alaskas

1 swiss roll
vanilla ice cream

1 tin drained fruit cocktail
2 egg whites
4 oz caster sugar

Pre-heat the oven to M8—450°. Slice the swiss roll in thick slices. On each slice place a scoop of vanilla ice cream, top with the drained fruit cocktail and spoon over the meringue made by stiffly beating the egg whites with the caster sugar. Pull into peaks with a fork and flash-bake for 2-3 minutes.

A. J. Cronin

strawberry mousse

1 packet of frozen strawberries
8 fluid ounces double cream

3 leaves gelatine
sugar to taste

'I am pleased to add my favourite recipe to your distinguished collection. It is Strawberry Mousse, as made by my good housekeeper who has been with me for thirty four years.'

Soak gelatine in cold water for a few minutes. Heat juice from strawberries with a little water and sugar to taste. Put gelatine in bowl, pour on hot juice, stir till melted. Put strawberries through a fine sieve and add. Let stand for 2 or 3 hours till just setting, beat with an egg beater till fluffy. Whip cream (not too stiff) and fold into mixture. Place in a decorative bowl, cover and leave in refrigerator for at least 24 hours.

Eric Sykes

big bad mouse

7-oz tin of sweetened chestnut purée   4 fluid ounces double cream
4 cartons of apricot yoghurt

'This is absolutely delicious — but rotten for dieters!'

Mix the chestnut purée and yoghurt well together. Beat the cream until fairly firm and fold into the mixture. Chill before serving. (Serves 6.)

Hattie Jacques

pineapple surprise

1 large pineapple   2 oz icing sugar
 (choose one that will stand upright) kirsch or brandy to taste
½ pint double cream

Take the lid off the pineapple, scoop out the fruit, cut into small pieces and drain off the juice. Beat the cream until thick, fold in the sugar and pineapple. Add the liqueur and pile all back into the pineapple shell. Put into fridge, also the excess filling to replenish pineapple.

Serve well-chilled with top replaced. (Serves 6-8.)

Lord Willis

for the batter
¼ lb flour
1 egg
½ pint milk
pinch of salt

fruit for the fritters
2 large apples or
slices of fresh pineapples or
bananas (not too ripe)

apple fritters

Sieve the flour and salt into a mixing bowl and make a well in the middle. Into this put the egg whole, and a little of the milk and mix well with a wooden spoon, adding more milk and working in the flour so as to keep the mixture smooth and thickish. After you have stirred in half of the milk, beat the batter for five minutes and put it aside in a cool place for an hour. Then smoothly stir in the rest of the milk.

Peel and core the apples and cut into quarter-inch thick rings. Drop each of these into the fritter batter and when well coated lift each ring out by means of the hole in the middle and drop into hot fat or oil, browning lightly on each side.

Serve sprinkled with caster sugar. If using bananas, peel them and slice them lengthways.

Emlyn Williams

pears dolores

6 ripe pears
1 tablespoon brown sugar
½ pint of orange juice (freshly squeezed)
juice of half a lemon

¼ pint of curaçao
red colouring
1 pint of vanilla ice cream

Peel the pears and slice them thinly into a serving bowl, sprinkle with sugar, add the juices, curaçao and a little colouring (just enough to tint the sauce slightly.) Marinate in the refrigerator for at least an hour before serving with vanilla ice cream. (Serves 4-6.)

Emlyn Williams

Cliff Michelmore

grapes marrinan

1 lb white grapes
whipped cream

soft brown sugar

'This is certainly a great favourite with the Michelmore household, and although this sounds extravagant white grapes are cheap when in season, and the only expensive ingredient is the cream.'

Peel and pip the grapes. Place in a fireproof dish and cover with a layer of whipped cream, top with the sugar and chill in refrigerator. Just before serving, place under a hot grill and remove just before the sugar catches fire.

Ronnie Barker

grape special

1 lb seedless grapes
   (if unavailable, de-pipping is essential)
½ pint double cream

large block vanilla ice cream
soft brown sugar

'This is a recipe that I and my family particularly enjoy. It is simple, but delicious.'

Put grapes into a fireproof dish, cover with the cream, and put into fridge *overnight*. About 10 or 12 minutes before the dish is required, light grill. Cover the grapes and cream with thick slices of ice cream, then cover ice cream with at least a ¼ inch of brown sugar, making sure no ice cream is showing through. Put under a very hot grill until the surface of the sugar is sizzling. A few seconds after removing from the grill, the sugar will cool and form a toffee apple-type surface over the whole dish.

Leslie Crowther

bread mountain

½ lb white bread
½ pint red wine
8 oz sugar (granulated)
thinly peeled rind of half a lemon
½ teaspoon cinnamon

3 eggs
fat for frying
apricot jam
6 oz caster sugar

Cut the bread into fingers and put into a bowl. Put the wine, granulated sugar, cinnamon and lemon peel into a small pan and bring slowly to the boil. Beat the egg yolks over heat until thick, then add the wine mixture, stirring all the time. Strain over the bread and leave for about 15 minutes. Brown the fingers of bread in hot fat and when cold spread with the jam. Pile into a heap on a dish and cover with the whisked egg whites and caster sugar, reserving some of the sugar to sprinkle over the top. Bake in a slow oven (M2—300°) until it is a golden-brown colour.

Believe me, this is delicious!

110

Doris Hare

crème brulée

1 pint double cream
1 split vanilla pod
4 egg yolks
4 to 5 tablespoons caster sugar

Set oven at M3—325°. Put the cream and vanilla pod in the top of a double boiler, cover and bring to scalding point. Meanwhile work egg yolks and one tablespoon of the sugar together with a wooden spoon until light in colour. Remove vanilla pod and pour the cream on to the egg yolks and sugar, and mix well. Return mixture to the pan and thicken very carefully over the heat, stirring continuously. The mixture should coat the wooden spoon, but on no account allow it to boil. Strain the mixture into a shallow ovenproof dish and place in the pre-set oven for 5-8 minutes, until a skin forms on top. Allow the cream to stand in a cool place for several hours, or preferably overnight.

Pre-heat the grill. Dust top of cream evenly with remaining sugar and slip it under grill at least 4 inches away from the heat. At this distance the sugar has a chance to melt before it begins to brown, and an even coating of caramel over the cream is ensured. Remove the cream from under the grill and let it stand in the refrigerator for 2-3 hours before serving.

Frankie Howerd

orange meringues

6 large oranges
3 oz cornflour
7 oz caster sugar
4 eggs

'The dessert is my favourite part of the meal (which is the reason why I'm always having to watch my weight). This is absolutely superb.'

Pre-heat oven (M4—350°). Cut oranges into halves, carefully squeeze juice, then strain into a measuring jug and make up to one pint with water if necessary. Scoop out all the pith from inside orange cups, cut edge of each orange cup with scissors to make zig-zag edges. Place on a baking sheet.

Place cornflour and 4 oz caster sugar in a saucepan, gradually add ¼ pint water and mix until smooth. Stir in about ½ pint of the orange juice and bring to boil, stirring continuously. Cook until cornflour has cleared and thickened, then remove from heat. Gradually stir remaining orange juice into cornflour mixture.

Separate eggs. Place whites in a clean grease-free bowl. Beat egg yolks into orange mixture, and stir over a moderate heat until mixture boils, spoon mixture into orange cups. Whisk egg whites until stiff with the remaining 3 oz of sugar. Divide the meringue between the orange cups and spread meringue to edge of each with the back of a spoon, then pull up meringue to form peaks. Place in centre of oven and bake for 15 minutes. Place on a serving dish and leave in a cool place. (Serves 12.)

Wendy Hiller
prune fool syllabub

½ lb of large prunes
¼ lb raisins
2 oz currants

¼ pint red wine or ⅛ pint port
(teetotallers use black coffee)
chopped almonds (optional)

Put prunes into an earthenware dish with wine and water to cover, and leave in a very slow oven (M1—275°) for 2-3 hours until quite soft. The raisins and currants, well-washed, are put in a separate pot in water, to bake for one hour. The prunes are sieved and mixed with the sieved and puréed raisins and currants. Add the chopped almonds. The purée mustn't be *too* solid.

Serve chilled with single cream and shortbread.

Judi Dench
orange syllabub

2 small oranges
½ lemon
2 oz caster sugar

½ pint double cream
grated orange rind

Finely grate the rind from one orange into a basin. Add the strained juice of both oranges and the lemon juice. Add sugar and stir until dissolved. Add cream and whisk until mixture is thick. Pour into individual glasses. Decorate with grated rind from the remaining peel. Chill and serve. (Serves 6.)

Spike Milligan

spaghettini special

1 lb spaghettini
1 carton double cream

caster sugar to taste
a dash of brandy

'I have a recipe which I made up myself, so I will give it to you.'

Cook the spaghettini in the normal way but do not add salt. Whip the double cream, add the caster sugar and brandy, then pour this over the spaghettini.

Adam Faith

treacle pudding (1)

for the pudding
8 oz self-raising flour
4 oz margarine
4 oz caster sugar
⅛ – ¼ pint of milk
1 egg
pinch of salt

for the sauce
warmed treacle
a few drops of lemon juice

Sieve flour and salt, rub in fat. Add sugar. Stir in lightly beaten egg and enough milk to make a fairly stiff mixture. Grease a baking dish, spread treacle over it and pour over the mixture. Place in a pre-heated oven (M5—375°) till golden brown.

Serve with the warmed treacle and lemon juice.

Evelyn Laye

treacle pudding (2)

for the pudding
4 oz flour
4 oz fresh breadcrumbs
½ teaspoon salt
4 oz suet, chopped or shredded
2 oz sugar
about ½ pint liquid to mix
    (this can be orange juice and water)
1 teaspoon baking powder

for the sauce
2 tablespoons treacle
1 tablespoon honey
grated rind of an orange

'This recipe will not make me very popular with slimmers, but as a rare — a very rare treat — it really is my favourite.'

Sieve the flour, baking powder and salt into a basin. If fresh suet is used, chop or shred it very finely. Mix all dry ingredients together in the basin. Make a well in the centre and add sufficient liquid to give a soft dropping consistency.

Into the bottom of a greased basin put in the sauce ingredients. Add the pudding mixture (filling the basin two-thirds full). Cover with greased paper. Steam steadily for two hours or longer. Turn out on to a hot dish.

Herbert Lom

8 trifle sponge cakes
cherry jam
2 full glasses of sherry (medium or sweet)
a rich custard made with 6 egg yolks
     and ¾ pint of milk
blobs of cream
ratafia biscuits
blanched almonds
glacé cherries (optional)

'real trifle'

'This is no kid's stuff with jelly and fruit! If I am holidaying in Tenerife I go out into my garden, pick a few ripe bananas and add them — peeled and sliced — to the sponge cake just before I pour on the custard — otherwise the banana slices will turn black. They must be covered completely and quickly.'

Spread the sponge cakes with the jam and arrange them in a dish and soak them with the sherry. Pour the custard over them. Allow to cool and decorate with the cream, blanched almonds and the cherries if used.

Serve with the ratafia biscuits.

Arnold Wesker

for the base
sponge cake soaked in brandy
chocolate-tipped sponge fingers

for the trifle
any flavour jelly
sliced orange and apple
nuts
custard flavoured with vanilla essence
flaked chocolate
sliced bananas
double cream
marron glacé purée

trifle

Lay the sponge cake soaked in brandy at the bottom of a glass bowl. Prop chocolate-tipped sponge fingers round the side. Add the layer of jelly, and just before jelly sets distribute the sliced orange, apple and nuts.

When jelly has set add a layer of custard. Just before custard sets distribute the flaked chocolate and sliced bananas.

When custard has set, place another layer of sponge cake soaked in brandy, and on top of this add a mixture of double cream whipped together with marron glacé purée. Decorate top to your fancy.

Arnold Wesker

117

Michael Aspel

lemon sponge soufflé

1½ oz butter
1 teacup sugar
2 tablespoons flour

2 eggs
rind and juice of one lemon
1 teacup milk

Cream butter together with the sugar, add the beaten egg yolks, lemon juice and rind of the lemon, and then fold in flour and the milk. Whip the egg whites until they are stiff and gently fold into the mixture, pour into a pudding dish and bake for approximately 40 minutes at M3—325°.

The pudding separates into two layers — a spongy cake on top and a bottom layer of creamy lemon sauce.

Sir Michael Balcon

ginger cream cold soufflé

½ jar of ginger in syrup, cut in thin slices
7 oz caster sugar
6 egg yolks

8 egg whites
½ pint whipped cream

Stir slowly in a bain-marie the sugar, egg yolks and ginger syrup. Pour into a basin. Add the whipped cream (not too stiff), the cut up ginger and finally fold in the stiffly beaten egg whites. Pour into a soufflé dish. Decorate with a little cream and ginger. Refrigerate until ready to serve. (Serves 6.)

cakes and biscuits

Bing Crosby

cream of orange pie

for the pastry
6 oz plain flour
4 oz butter or margarine
2 level teaspoons caster sugar
1½ oz ground almonds
1 egg yolk
1 tablespoon water

for the filling
6 tablespoons finely cut orange marmalade
½ pint double cream
3 egg yolks
2 level teaspoons cornflour

Sift the flour into a bowl and rub in the fat. Add the sugar and ground almonds. Separate the egg and blend yolk with the water. Stir this into the rubbed-in ingredients. Knead lightly and roll out on a cool, floured surface. Line a 9-inch loose-bottomed French fluted flan tin with it and cover with aluminium foil, pressing lightly into the sides. Bake blind for 15 minutes at M5—375°. Remove foil and cook for a further 5 minutes. Allow to cool slightly.

Blend the 3 egg yolks with the cornflour and the cream. Spread the marmalade over the base of the flan case and cover with the cream mixture. Make a lattice of strips from the pastry trimmings and lay them gently on top. Bake for 20 minutes at M6—400° until the filling is firm and golden brown. Leave to cool in the tin before turning out.

Bob Hope

1 baked flan case
1 cup sugar plus 2 tablespoons
3 tablespoons cornflour
1 cup of boiling water
4 tablespoons lemon juice

2 tablespoons butter
4 eggs
pinch of salt
grated rind of 1 lemon and the juice

favourite lemon pie

Combine the cornflour and the cup of sugar, add the boiling water slowly, stirring constantly until thick and smooth. Add the slightly beaten egg yolks, butter, lemon rind, lemon juice and salt. Cook for 2 or 3 minutes. Pour into the flan case. Cover with meringue made from the egg whites stiffly beaten and the 2 tablespoons sugar. Bake in a slow oven for 15 minutes, or until the meringue is golden brown.

Dame Flora Robson

balkan honey pie

for the pastry
4 oz flour
4 oz butter
iced water

for the filling
½ lb cottage cheese
2 oz honey (2 tablespoons)
2 oz caster sugar
2 eggs
cinnamon

'This is a delightful flan, and as I am an amateur cook, I am proud to say it always turns out well.'

Make the pastry and line the flan case with it. Chill. Soften the cottage cheese, add the sugar, the beaten eggs and honey. Mix well. Pour into the flan case, sprinkle cinnamon on the surface. Bake for 30-35 minutes at M5—375°.

Flora Robson

122

Irene Handl
chocolate cake

for the cake
4 oz unsalted butter
4 oz caster sugar
almond essence
grated rinds of ½ lemon and ½ orange
small pinch of cinnamon
2 tiny pinches ground cloves
2 oz plain chocolate
4 oz ground almonds
2 large eggs
2 teaspoons brandy or rum
2 oz self-raising flour

for the coating and icing
small quantity orange marmalade
small quantity rum or brandy
4 oz plain chocolate
small nut of butter

Grease and dust with plain flour a loaf tin measuring 9 x 5 inches. Cream the butter and sugar together in a basin until very light in colour, add a few drops of almond essence, the rinds and the spices. Soften the chocolate and stir it into the mixture together with the ground almonds. Whisk the eggs well together and add to the mixture, a little at a time, together with a little of the flour and the rum or brandy. (The flour prevents the mixture curdling after the addition of spirit.) Finally fold in the remainder of the flour with a metal spoon until evenly blended. Turn mixture into a prepared tin, smooth top, and bake for 45-55 minutes at M4—350°.

When the cake is cooked, it will have shrunk a little from the sides of the tin. Turn it out on to a wire cooling tray and allow it to get quite cold, then brush the cake all over with the orange marmalade which has been thinned down with a little brandy or rum.

Soften the chocolate with a little hot water, and place the basin over a pan of hot (*not boiling*) water. When very smooth and thick, remove the pan from the heat and beat in a small nut of butter. When just warm and very glossy, pour over the cake and allow to set.

This cake keeps very well in an airtight tin.

Sir Charles Clore mocha cake

for the cake
4 oz butter
4 oz caster sugar
2 eggs
4 oz plain flour
pinch of salt
¾ teaspoon baking powder
2 teaspoons coffee essence

for the butter icing
6 oz icing sugar
3 oz butter
little rum flavouring
little powdered coffee

for the coffee icing
icing sugar
warm strong black coffee

Cream together the butter and sugar, then beat in the eggs one at a time. Add the sifted flour, salt, baking powder and coffee essence and stir lightly. Put into a greased and lined 6-inch diameter cake tin. Bake for 55 minutes at M4—350°. When the cake is cold cut through the middle, spread with most of the butter icing. Ice the top of the cake with coffee icing. Decorate with the remains of the butter icing.

Butter icing. Beat the sugar and butter to a light cream. Add the rum and coffee to taste.

Coffee icing. Mix the icing sugar with the black coffee, until the icing begins to thicken. Pour over cake and spread with a wet palette knife.

Baroness Spencer Churchill chocolate cake

½ lb butter
7 eggs
½ lb plain vanilla-flavoured chocolate
3 oz plain flour

½ lb sifted icing sugar
4 oz ground almonds
1 teaspoon sal volatile

Beat the butter to a cream. Beat the egg yolks and stir into the butter, then beat and stir in the stiffly whipped egg whites. Scrape the chocolate and melt it in the oven (or in a small bowl standing within a saucepan of hot water). Gently fold this into the mixture, together with all the other ingredients. Bake in a slow oven (M3—325°) for 45-50 minutes. Keep for two or three days before eating. A thin icing of soft white sugar, flavoured with lemon, will keep the cake deliciously moist.

Brian Rix

hot bread cake

1 lb 5 oz plain flour
1 oz yeast
2½ oz butter
3 oz caster sugar
4 egg yolks
1 teaspoon vanilla
1 tablespoon rum or brandy (or more, to taste)
grated rind of 1 lemon
some cold milk
1 whole egg

'I don't know whether this is a bread or a cake. I suppose the answer depends on what it is served with. It is so easy to bake, that even husbands cannot help but succeed when they try.'

Mix a dough of the flour, yeast, butter, sugar, egg yolks, vanilla essence, rum or brandy, lemon rind with cold milk, and knead well. Put aside to rise for half an hour. Cut into four quarters and form small loaves which are put on a buttered baking sheet to rise for two hours more. *Do not* add any raisins, sultanas or currants. With a very sharp knife, cut a 'Y' into the surface and brush it several times with the well-beaten whole egg. The loaves should be started in a pre-warmed moderate oven and the heat reduced to M1—275° shortly afterwards.

Half an hour later you should be rewarded with tempting shiny brown soft loaves of bread/cake. It makes out-of-this-world toast, and tastes marvellous with butter and/or cream cheese.

Dahlia Lavi

cheese cake

for the base
crushed biscuits
2 oz butter

for the filling
1 lb cooking cream cheese
3 eggs
4 oz caster sugar
2 tubs sour cream
1 tin strained fruit cocktail (optional)

Mix the crushed biscuits with the melted butter, and moisten down well into the tin. Mix the cheese, eggs, 3 oz of the sugar, and beat together until free of lumps. Pour onto the base. Bake for 20 minutes at M5—375°. Remove from oven and cool slightly. Mix the remaining sugar with the sour cream, pour it on top of the cheese and bake for a further 7-10 minutes to set.

If using the fruit cocktail, mix with the sour cream and sugar before replacing in the oven.

Leslie Grade

strawberry flan chantilly

1 lb strawberries
6 tablespoons Grand Marnier
sugar to taste

1 egg white
½ pint whipped cream
1 baked flan case

Wash, hull and slice the strawberries into a bowl. Pour Grand Marnier over them. Add sugar to taste, stir gently and let marinate for 30 minutes. Beat the egg white until stiff and fold into the whipped cream. Just before serving, fold the sliced strawberries into the cream and pile into the baked flan case.

Shirley Bassey

plum cake

9 oz butter
8 oz caster sugar
12 oz self-raising flour
5 eggs

9 oz candied plums
    (or glacé cherries can also be used)
8 oz candied citron
8 oz currants
¼ pint brandy

Cream the butter with the sugar, then mix in 10 ounces of the flour, and then the 5 eggs. Use the remaining 2 oz flour for coating the candied fruits, which should then all be gently stirred into the mixture. Add the brandy and pour the dough into a large square cake tin. Bake in a pre-heated oven (M4—350°) for approximately 1½ hours.

Georges Simenon

tarte aux poireaux

for the tarte
6 oz plain flour
4 oz butter
2 level teaspoons caster sugar
2 oz ground almonds
1 egg yolk
few drops almond essence
1 tablespoon ice-cold water

for the filling
1 lb pears
butter
sugar to taste

'This recipe is a French one and the pastry can be made well in advance.'

Sift the flour into a bowl, add the sugar and ground almonds and rub in the fat until the mixture resembles fine breadcrumbs. Stir in the egg yolk, water and almond essence. Knead lightly and roll out on to a cool, floured surface. Line a 9-inch loose-bottomed flan tin with it, pressing lightly into the sides of the tin with the pastry. Bake blind for 15 minutes.

Meanwhile peel and core the pears and cut them into small pieces. Cook for a few moments in butter with a little sugar to taste. Spread the cooked pears over the flan base and place in the oven (M6—400°) until it is golden brown on top.

Rose Kennedy

boston cream pie

for the cream sponge cake
4 eggs
1 cup granulated sugar
1½ tablespoons lemon juice
1 cup pastry flour
1¼ teaspoons baking powder
pinch of salt
1 teaspoon vanilla essence
1½ tablespoons cold water

for the icing
3 tablespoons cornflour
2-3 cups granulated sugar
pinch of salt
3 egg yolks
1½ cups scalded milk
2 tablespoons butter
1 teaspoon vanilla essence
sifted icing sugar

Cake. Sift the flour 3 times. Beat the egg whites until stiff but not dry, and fold in half the quantity of sugar gradually. Beat egg yolks and liquids and continue to beat until very thick and pale yellow. Beat in the remaining sugar. Combine yolks and whites, folding together until mixture is well blended. Mix and sift in flour, baking powder and salt, cutting and folding into the egg mixture. Pour into a buttered tin. Bake in a slow oven (M3−325°) for 1 hour.

Split the cream sponge cake into 2 layers after it has been kept 24 hours. Mix the cornflour, sugar and salt. Beat egg yolks until thick and combine with cornflour mixture, beating until perfectly smooth. Pour on hot milk gradually, add butter and vanilla. Cook in the top of a double boiler until thick, stirring all the time to prevent lumping. Spread between the cake layers and sift icing sugar on top of the cake.

Donald Sinden

apple pie

for the pastry
8 oz plain or self-raising flour
pinch of salt
5 oz margarine
1 tablespoon iced water

for the filling
1 tablespoon flour
juice and rind of half a lemon
4 tablespoons caster sugar
1 lb cooking apples
¼ pint double cream

'My favourite recipe is for a superbly-cooked apple pie with a touch of lemon and no cloves. For this dish I will travel — and have travelled — anywhere.'

Pastry. Sieve the flour and salt into a mixing bowl. Add the margarine and rub in with the fingertips until the mixture looks like fine breadcrumbs. Mix in the water with the blade of a knife to form a firm dough. Turn out on to a floured board, roll out pastry to fit a deep 8-inch pie dish, and bake in a pre-heated oven (M5—375°) for 15 minutes.

Filling. Mix the flour, lemon juice, rind and sugar together. Peel, core and cut the apples into thin slices. Toss them in the flour and place them in the baked pastry case. Sprinkle a little flour over the apple slices, then pour over the double cream. Bake in a moderate oven (M4—350°) on middle shelf for 40-45 minutes. Serve hot.

Jackie Stewart
lemon meringue pie

for the pastry
6 oz plain flour
4 oz butter
1 egg yolk
¾ oz caster sugar
2 teaspoons cold water
good pinch of salt

for the filling
2 large lemons
1½ oz cornflour
½ pint water
2 egg yolks
3 oz caster sugar

for the meringue
3 egg whites
5 oz caster sugar

Sift flour and salt into a mixing bowl. Cut the butter in small pieces and coat with the flour. Rub in with fingertips until the mixture resembles fine breadcrumbs. Stir in the sugar, mix the egg yolk with water and mix with a knife to a firm dough. Turn on to a floured board and knead lightly until smooth. If possible, chill for 30 minutes before use. Line an 8-inch flan ring with the pastry. Prick base with a fork and leave in a cold place for 20 minutes. Fill with a piece of crumpled foil and dried beans and bake blind in a hot oven (M7—425°) for 15 minutes. Remove paper and beans.

Put grated lemon rind and juice in a bowl with the cornflour. Add two tablespoons water and blend until smooth. Boil remaining water and pour into the cornflour mixture. Return mixture to pan, bring to boil and simmer for 3 minutes until thick. Remove from heat and add egg yolks and sugar. Cool slightly then spoon into flan case.

To make the meringue. Whisk the egg whites until stiff and dry. Whisk in two teaspoons of the sugar and then fold in the remainder with a metal spoon. Pipe meringue over the lemon filling. Bake in a moderate oven (M4—350°) for 15 minutes. (Serves 6.)

A very pleasant variation is to replace the lemons with two oranges.

Lady Bird Johnson
prune cake

for the cake
½ cup of shortening
1 cup of caster sugar
2 eggs
1⅓ cups of flour
⅔ cup of chopped prunes
⅔ cup of sour milk
½ teaspoon salt
½ teaspoon cinnamon
½ teaspoon nutmeg
½ teaspoon allspice
½ teaspoon baking powder

for the frosting
2 tablespoons butter
2 tablespoons prune juice
1 tablespoon lemon juice
½ teaspoon cinnamon
½ teaspoon salt
1½ cups icing sugar

Cream shortening, add sugar and eggs and beat well. Mix all the dry ingredients and add alternately with the sour milk to the creamed mixture. Add chopped prunes. Bake in 2 waxed paper-lined cake tins for about 25 minutes at M4—350°.

Cream butter, add prune and lemon juices, salt and cinnamon. Beat in icing sugar gradually. Sandwich the two cakes together with this.

Richard Nixon

raspberry pie

two 10 oz packets of frozen raspberries, thawed
2 cups vanilla wafer crumbs
½ cup caster sugar
1 teaspoon cinnamon
5 tablespoons melted butter
1 envelope of unflavoured gelatine
¼ cup cold water
½ teaspoon grated lemon peel
½ pint double cream
1 teaspoon vanilla essence

Drain the raspberries, reserving one cup of the juice. Combine the crumbs, sugar, half a teaspoon of the cinnamon and the butter and pat into a 10-inch pie plate. Bake in a pre-heated oven (M5–375°) for 8-10 minutes, let cool.

Soften gelatine in the cold water. Mix the reserved raspberry juice, the remaining half a teaspoon of cinnamon and the grated lemon peel, and heat to boiling. Remove from heat, add the gelatine and stir until melted. Chill until the mixture just begins to thicken.

Whip cream and vanilla essence. Fold in the raspberries and gelatine mixture. Pour into the pie shell and chill.

When serving, decorate with additional whipped cream if desired.

Russ Conway

swedish nut wafers

2½ oz butter
6 oz caster sugar
1 well beaten egg
3 dessertspoons milk
little vanilla essence
6 oz plain flour
1 level teaspoon baking powder
½ level teaspoon salt
1 teacup chopped nuts

Cream butter together with sugar till white. Add the egg, milk, vanilla essence, then the flour sieved with baking powder and salt. Spread thinly on an *inverted* baking tin, sprinkle with chopped nuts, and mark in strips ¾ of an inch wide. Bake in a moderate oven about 10-12 minutes. Cut through the strips and shape them over a rolling pin. They will harden as they cool into bracelet shapes. If the strips get too brittle, return to oven to soften.

confectionery and non-bake cakes

Roger Moore

chocolate refrigerator cake

2 lb small digestive biscuits
½ lb butter
8 tablespoons golden syrup
½ lb plain chocolate
grated rind of 1 lemon
grated rind of 1 orange
4 oz chopped nuts

for decoration
½ lb plain chocolate

Grease and line a 9-10 inch loose-based cake tin. Put ½ lb biscuits to one side and crush the remainder. Melt butter, golden syrup, and chocolate. Stir in grated rinds, nuts and the crushed biscuits. Spoon into the prepared tin and place in the refrigerator to set. Carefully take the cake from the tin and place on a serving dish. Melt the chocolate reserved for the decoration, place the ½ lb biscuits around the sides of the cake slightly overlapping, and secure with a little chocolate. Spoon remaining chocolate over top of cake, swirl decoratively.

John Le Mesurier
malakoff

1 lb sponge fingers
6 oz chocolate
1 tablespoon sugar
2 eggs

1 carton double cream
red wine or black coffee
chopped nuts

Dip the sponge fingers in the diluted red wine or black coffee and line a cake tin with them — bottom and sides. Mix the egg yolks with the sugar and melted chocolate and 2 spoons of black coffee. When cold, add the beaten egg whites and pour over the sponge fingers. Cover with whipped cream and top with the chopped nuts.

Joan Sims
quick biscuit cake

8 oz digestive biscuits
1 oz caster sugar
4 oz margarine

1 tablespoon golden syrup
3 level tablespoons cocoa
cooking chocolate for topping

Crush biscuits finely between two sheets of paper. Melt the sugar, margarine and golden syrup together over a low heat. Cool for a few moments then beat in the biscuit crumbs. Add the cocoa and beat again. Line a sandwich tin with foil, press the crumb mixture into it and pat down firmly. Leave in the fridge to set. Top with melted cooking chocolate.

Sacha Distel

apricot fancies

8 oz stale cake crumbs
4 rounded tablespoons apricot jam
1 oz butter or margarine
3 to 4 heaped tablespoons dessicated coconut
halved walnuts
blanched almonds
glacé cherries

Crumble the cake into very fine crumbs. Heat the jam with the butter or margarine, stirring well. Add some of the jam to the crumbs and mix to a firm paste with a wooden spoon, blending well.

Take heaped teaspoons of the mixture and form into small balls between the palms of the hand. Drop into remaining warm jam to coat. Lift out with a fork, drain off surplus jam, then roll in dessicated coconut placed on a plate. Press in half a walnut, or glacé cherry etc. on top of each ball to decorate. Leave in a cool place until set.

miscellaneous

Michael Flanders
recipe for happiness

1 bottle Evian water
1 apple

1 peanut butter, marmite and cress sandwich

To be eaten by the sea!

Liberace
hot spiced punch

½ cup brown sugar
½ cup granulated sugar
1 quart orange juice
1 cup lemon juice

1 pint apple juice
two 2-inch sticks of cinnamon
3 whole cloves
orange slices and curls of lemon peel
    for decoration

Boil apple juice together with the sugars, cinnamon and cloves for 5 minutes. Add the orange and lemon juices which have previously been heated just to boiling point.

Serve in pottery bowls and garnish with slices of orange and lemon peel curls.

Jimmy Savile
millionaire munch

porridge oats   **treacle**

Mix together porridge oats and treacle, leave several days and consume first thing in the morning. This puts you off food for the rest of the day and the money you save makes you a millionaire. God bless!

Dr. Benjamin Spock
quick cooking porridge

for each person: **pinch of salt**
2-3 heaped tablespoons quick porridge oats **sugar to taste**
½ cup milk or milk and water   **a dab of butter**

Mix everything together, bring to the boil and let boil for 1 minute stirring all the time. Cover the saucepan and let stand for approximately 5 minutes. This can be served with honey and for a change any kind of sliced fruit can be added.

Yehudi Menuhin

5 fresh fertilized eggs laid by free happy hens
$2^2/_3$ cups rich (unpasteurized) cream
$2^2/_3$ cups home-made yoghurt
3 or 4 heaped tablespoons non-instant skim
    milk powder
1 heaped tablespoon brewers' yeast powder
    (does not improve flavour but is meritorious)
2 tablespoons cold-pressed safflower oil
    (if Vitamin E oil available or almond oil,
    use as well)
4 tablespoons honey
juice of ½-1 whole orange
Best old Napoleon Brandy — sufficient to mask
    virtue!

santa's claws egg nog

Prepare ingredients in four bowls:

In one bowl beat egg whites until stiff.

In a second bowl beat egg yolks adding orange juice and (gradually) oil until emulsified.

In third bowl beat cream and then add yoghurt, milk powder, yeast and honey.*

Empty all three bowls into the fourth (largest!) bowl, adding brandy and orange juice to taste.

Serves 4 (in 8 small glasses).

---

* The following ingredients can also be added to the third bowl if desired: lecithin, calcium gluconate or lactate, magnesium oxide, soy flour, wheat germ and nutmeg (kelp).

Sam Wanamaker

pear preserve

4 lb hard pears
3 lb granulated sugar
finely grated rind and juice of 2 lemons

2 level teaspoons cinnamon
6 cloves
small glass brandy

Peel pears, cut them in halves and remove cores with a knife. Put the halves into a basin and sprinkle them with the sugar, lemon juice and lemon rind. Leave overnight. Next day add the cinnamon and cloves.

Pack the preserves into a large oven-proof casserole and place in a slow oven (M2—300°) till pears are tender. This will normally take about 6 hours. Take the casserole out of the oven, pour in the brandy to taste, and leave to cool.

Transfer into jam jars and cover with polythene. Keep for three months before use.

Freda Riseman

gin fizz

a little gin
juice of half a lemon
a thin strip of lemon rind

1 dessertspoon caster sugar
1 egg white
a few ice cubes

'Finally, as compiler of this book, may I take this opportunity to toast all my distinguished contributors and readers with my favourite cocktail recipe.'

Place all the ingredients in a liquidizer or cocktail shaker and blend for about 20-30 seconds. Strain into two long glasses and fill with soda water.

index of contributors

144